Cooking the One-Burner Way

Gourmet Cuisine for the Backcountry Chef

Help Us Keep This Guide Up to Date

Every effort has been made by the authors and editors to make this guide as accurate and useful as possible. However, many things can change after a guide is published—establishments close, phone numbers change, facilities come under new management, etc.

We would love to hear from you concerning your experiences with this guide and how you feel it could be improved and kept up to date. While we may not be able to respond to all comments and suggestions, we'll take them to heart and we'll also make certain to share them with the authors. Please send your comments and suggestions to the following address:

The Globe Pequot Press
Reader Response/Editorial Department
P.O. Box 480
Guilford, CT 06437

Or you may e-mail us at:

editorial@globe-pequot.com

Thanks for your input, and happy cooking!

Cooking the One-Burner Way

Gourmet Cuisine for the Backcountry Chef

SECOND EDITION

by Melissa Gray and Buck Tilton

The Globe Pequot Press

Guilford, Connecticut

Cover photos: Melissa Gray
Cover design: Adam Schwartzman
Text design: Nancy Freeborn

Library of Congress Cataloging-in-Publication Data
Gray, Melissa, 1960-
    Cooking the one-burner way : gourmet cuisine for the backcountry chef /
  by Melissa Gray and Buck Tilton.— [2nd ed.].
        p. cm.
    Includes index.
    ISBN 0-7627-0670-8
    1. Outdoor cookery. I. Tilton, Buck. II. Title.

TX823.G73 2000
641.5'78—dc21

                                                        00-021734

Manufactured in the United States of America
Second Edition/First Printing

Contents

To our moms, Elaine Dube and Eris Tilton, with great love and deep appreciation for the many years they fed us.

Acknowledgments

Books are seldom, if ever, the work of one or two people. An appeal to our friends for their favorite backcountry recipes, and other assistance, brought a foodbag of tasty responses. We especially thank: Kate Bartlett, Jerri Bell, Margaret Brady, Alexandra Conover, Kitty Ann and Roger Cox, Peter DeJung, Elaine Doll, Tamah Donaldson, Elaine Dube, Bethany Grohs and Justin Grohs, Barb Harper, Michael Hock, Ruthe Hubbell, Iretta Hunter, Lisa Jaeger, Cliff Jacobson, Brett LeCompte, Tim Lindhold, J. Scott McGee, Rob Meltzer, Steve Mital, Steve Platz and Shana Tarter, Daniel Robison, James Rosner, Jennifer Rouillard, Ben Sparks, Mark Stivers, Eris Tilton, David Tomco, Ronald Turner, Woodswomen, Inc., and, for tireless day-to-day effort, Lori "Spike" Patin.

Introduction

Not another outdoor cookbook! Well, yes . . . and no. Yes, even if you know how to cook outdoors, by the time you've digested all the information in this book you'll know how to cook outdoors better. So it's a cookbook. But, no, even if you know nothing about cooking outdoors, this book gives you all you need to know about choosing food and stoves and cook gear, about how much of what you'll need for so many days, about special considerations such as high altitude and extreme cold, about camp hygiene so you don't consume things that make you unhealthy, about leaving your campsite environmentally clean, and about preparing everything from Yippee-Ki-Yay Cowboy Coffee to Wild Currant Cottlestone Pie via your choice of entrees. In short, this book gives you the opportunity to become a backcountry chef.

This book sits firmly on a one-burner backcountry-stove foundation. One-burner because such stoves are available, lightweight, compact, and infinitely functional. Backcountry because Mother Earth has withstood too many open fires in too many places for too long a time. Although campfires are acceptable, or at least tolerated, in some places, with a one-burner you'll cook faster and be able to dine finely in areas with limited wood, such as above tree line. More and more backcountry chefs need to be taking only pictures and leaving only nothing.

Our longest one-burner trip was sixty-two days in Idaho's Frank Church–River of No Return Wilderness, where a small Cessna dropped our resupplies. The shortest was a one-nighter cooking off the tailgate of our Bronco, fishing the beaver ponds along Colorado's Middle Quartz Creek. In between lie over forty combined years of boiling, baking, poaching, and frying out of backpacks, canoe bags, sea-kayak bags, and saddle-bags. On many nights we've coaxed hot soup out of cold pots at 18,000 feet in Alaska and swatted mosquitoes while fresh fish sizzled in Florida. We've taught cooking to students from junior high schools, high schools, colleges, universities, Outward Bound, the National Outdoor Leadership School, the Wilderness Education Association, and the Boy Scouts.

Now here we sit on the eve of a new millennium, overjoyed about life, the universe, and everything—including the fact that *Cooking the One-Burner Way* is coming out in a second edition with updated information and a potful of new recipes.

Through hundreds and hundreds of backcountry days, we've progressed from solid lumps of scorched mac-and-cheese to fresh-baked bread and delicately seasoned casseroles. This book will make your journey much shorter . . . and far more tasty. In the end we hope you'll have more fun eating better and taking better care of the backcountry.

Melissa Gray and Buck Tilton
Pitkin, Colorado
November 1999

Nutrition:
Body Fuel

Food whatever its taste and psychological benefits, acts as fuel for the human engine. It's go-power, and the worth of the go is called its nutritional value. Nutrition, like politics, ends up being largely a matter of personal opinion, but a shortage of nutrients, despite who you voted for, causes everyone to have energy slumps that bring early fatigue, lassitude, mind numbness, and a predisposition for getting sick. Start every backcountry trip by planning to eat nutritionally well.

Energy Sources

Your body has three sources of energy: carbohydrates, fats, and, to some extent, proteins. Although all food ends up being digested into simple compounds before it can be burned for power, **carbohydrates** (sugars and starches) digest the quickest and easiest. Simple carbohydrates (simple sugars: table sugar, brown sugar, date sugar, honey, molasses) are small molecular units that break down very fast, entering the bloodstream soon after you eat them. You get an energy boost right away. But most sugars are burned so quickly that energy levels can suddenly fall below your starting point if all you eat is simple carbohydrates. So complex carbohydrates (strings of simple sugars called starches) need to be a major portion of your diet. Being a more complex molecular unit, starches break down more slowly, providing power for the long haul. Carbohydrates should supply at least 60 percent of the calories in your backcountry diet.

Complex Carbohydrate Sources: Whole grains and whole-grain products (cereals, breads), pasta, fruits, and vegetables.

Fat is necessary for a healthy life . . . but not much fat. In fact, your body will manufacture fat from carbohydrates and proteins if you run short. Your body worries about running out of fat so much that it'll store unbelievable quantities against a fatless day. Unfortunately and unhealthily, you don't know when you have too much of a good thing. Fat breaks down very slowly in the digestive process, so more time is required for it to provide energy. There are saturated fats and unsaturated

1

fats, and most fats, animal and vegetable, are combinations of both kinds. Saturated fats are harder and stick to your arteries better, and so they're considered less healthy than unsaturated fats. Cholesterol (lipoprotein) is a substance found in animal fats. Low-density lipoproteins (LDL) seem to lend themselves to heart disease more than high-density lipoproteins (HDL). HDLs have even been associated with a reduced risk of heart disease. Fats have a devilish quality: They tend to taste really good. But fats should supply only approximately 25 percent of your diet.

Fat Sources: Butter, margarine, oils, cheeses, meats, and nuts.

Proteins are made up of amino acids, and amino acids are the basic substance of human tissue. Proteins are not a primary energy source, but your body will use them if nothing else is available, or if you exercise for a long period of time. But since tissue is continually lost and replaced (and new tissue is built when you exercise), proteins are essential to life. All of the amino acids are synthesized by your body—except for eight, which have to be eaten. A "complete protein" has all eight of these amino acids. Eggs, milk, and meat (including fish) are complete. Other foods, such as grains, seeds, nuts, and legumes, contain incomplete proteins, but since they're incomplete in different ways, some of them can be combined to form complete proteins. Legumes (soybeans, navy beans, kidney beans, pinto beans, lima beans, peanuts, black-eyed peas, chickpeas, split peas, lentils) combine with seeds and nuts to form complete proteins, and milk products and whole grains combine completely also. Most whole grains combine with most legumes to complete the protein package. Some milk products combine with some seeds and nuts to form complete proteins. Proteins need to make up about 15 percent of your diet.

Protein Sources: Meat, milk and milk products, eggs, seeds, nuts, legumes, whole grains.

Boost your protein intake by:

Combining rice with legumes, wheat, seeds, or milk products. Check out Creamy Rice Pudding (see Desserts) or Quick Curried Rice (Entrees).

Combining wheat with legumes, nuts, seeds, or milk products. Check out Pizza (see Entrees) or Peanut Butter Bread (Backcountry Baking).

Combining legumes with corn, seeds, whole grains, or milk products. Check out Falafel and Cheese Tortillas (see Entrees).

Combining seeds with milk products. Check out "Szechwan" Noodles (see Entrees) or Barb's Granola (Breakfasts).

Combining potatoes and milk products. Check out Bugg's Alpine Start (see Breakfasts) or Spicy Shepard's Pie (Entrees).

Vitamins, Minerals, Fiber

You won't function for long without **vitamins,** and these little organic molecules must be eaten. Vitamins are necessary for food to be processed into energy for life. There are thirteen known vitamins. Some are fat soluble (A, D, E, K), and are stored in fatty tissue and organ tissue of the body. Some are water soluble (C and the Bs), cannot be stored, and wash out when you sweat or urinate. As long as you eat a balanced diet, you'll probably get the vitamins you need. On extended backcountry trips you may consider taking a daily multivitamin that meets the recommended daily allowances (RDA) of the National Academy of Sciences. To exceed the RDA, especially with fat-soluble vitamins, may be harmful.

Traces of several **minerals** are also required for you to continue to function. These minerals are generally divided into two classes: 1) major minerals (such as calcium) that you need more of than 2) minor minerals (such as iron). Once again, a balanced diet supplies all the minerals you need. If you decide to take supplements, do not exceed the RDA. Remember: Taking vitamin/mineral supplements is like trying to cheat your way to health. They are not a substitute for eating right.

Fiber is that stuff in some foods that you eat but don't digest, yet it plays a vital role in health. There are two kinds of fibers: insoluble (whole-grain products, bran, cellulose) and soluble (oats, oat bran, fruits, vegetables, nuts, beans). Insoluble fiber won't hold much water, so it moves quickly through your digestive tract and encourages other food to move quickly, keeping your bowel movements regular. Too much insoluble fiber may produce too much movement. Soluble fiber absorbs water and becomes gooey, sticking to other foods and slowing their assimilation into your body. This is healthy because soluble fibers stick to some potentially harmful cholesterol better than your body does, so it is carried out.

Water

Water probably ranks as the most common thing your body needs more of on a backcountry trip. It is the most important nutrient that passes your lips, something you need almost as critically as air, the medium of energy production and body temperature control and waste removal of metabolic by-products. To feel well and perform well, you've got to drink a lot of water, because you lose it constantly through sweat and urination and defecation, even through breathing.

Start each day with about a half quart, or sixteen ounces, of water. During periods of exercise you should be downing about eight more ounces every fifteen or twenty minutes. For wilderness travel, and for life in general, the old piece of advice to drink enough water to keep your urine clear and copious rings with truth . . . as long as you are also eating regularly.

Nutrition in the Cold Outdoors

Although your need for vitamins and minerals does not change in a cold environment, your need for water goes up and your energy requirements are increased. To meet the increased need, you should drink more and eat more. The single most important factor in cold-weather food consumption is carrying food you enjoy eating. The nutrient breakdown should be approximately the same: 60 percent carbohydrate, 25 percent fat, 15 percent protein. Carbohydrate intake is especially important to replenish muscle energy stores in order to prevent excess fatigue, which often leads to cold injury. Cold tolerance may be improved for most people by a high-fat snack (about one third the calories from fat) every couple of hours: one or two snacks between breakfast and lunch, another one between lunch and dinner, and one more before crawling into your sleeping bag. If you're one of those people who awaken cold during the night, pack a snack into your sleeping bag. We like to make a water bottle of hot chocolate before bedtime. In the sleeping bag it provides warmth by contact. Later in the night it provides warmth by calories. (Make sure the top is screwed on tight!)

Nutrition at High Altitude

Higher altitudes tend to be cold, and the same cold-weather recommendations apply, with one exception: Fat is not tolerated as well at higher altitudes—altitudes above 16,000 feet. Fat tolerances decrease as altitude increases. You will probably function better if you change high-fat snacks to high-energy, high-carbohydrate snacks. There is also some evidence indicating that people on high-carb diets—about 70 percent carbohydrate—acclimatize better to higher altitudes. Because altitude often affects your appetite, it is critical to carry food you crave. Proper nutrition is important, but not as important as an adequate caloric and fluid intake. And not as important as healthy physical conditioning, and proper clothing and gear.

Food and Menu Planning

General Thoughts

Whether it's a paddling weekend on the lakes of Minnesota or a month on a high Alaskan mountain, nothing upsets people faster than having too little or rotten-tasting food. Too much can also be a problem, especially if you're required to carry it or pull it, but it doesn't usually result in the death of the food packer/cook.

So here's some questions to ask yourself and your traveling companions before purchasing an packing the grub.

1. **HOW LONG WILL YOU BE IN THE BACKCOUNTRY?** For short trips (less than a week), we tend to count the specific meals needed, preplan a menu, and repackage ingredients into a Bag-a-Feast per meal. On longer trips we package our food in bulk bags and plan our menus as we go. Both of these methods will be described in greater detail later in this chapter.

2. **WHAT'S THE TIME OF YEAR AND LEVEL OF EXPECTED ACTIVITY?** Cold weather and high-intensity exercise will increase the caloric need of your body. Are you planning to fish or hunt? Fish can be a great supplement to a diet, but if you get skunked you can be very hungry. Trust us, it happens!

3. **WHO'S GOING WITH YOU?** A coed group of pre-adolescents eats far less than a group of guys in their twenties. Most small folks eat less than most large folks. People experienced with outdoor cooking and travel tend to eat more than novices (instructors versus students). Some people just plain eat more than other people. When packing for groups, this usually evens out somewhere; otherwise, "practice makes perfect."

4. **DOES THE GROUP HAVE ANY SPECIAL NEEDS?** Allergies, diabetes, religion, and even likes and dislikes greatly affect what people will eat. An informal questionnaire is often helpful.

5. **HOW MUCH MONEY DO YOU HAVE?** Yes, you must have a certain amount, but by staying away from prepacked meals and specialty items you sure save dollars as well as cutting down on wasteful packaging.

Total Ration Planning Versus Specific Menu Planning

Basically you have two options for food and menu planning. We use them both regularly but in different situations.

Option 1: Total Ration Planning

Total Ration Planning is our first choice for backcountry food planning. It works just as well for two folks on a ten-day Maine coastal kayaking trip as it does for a group of twelve backpackers crossing Utah's Grand Gulch.

Total Ration Planning grants you the freedom to pack a wide variety of dried foods, allowing for endless meal options. When you menu-plan as you go, instead of ahead of time, you are allowed to be spontaneous, adapting to the day's preferences and tasks. Food requirements change easily with the weather and your preferences.

Also, by cooking from scratch you minimize prepackaged foods, increase nutrition, cut down on fat and salt, get to use your imagination, and, most important, impress your companions with your cooking prowess.

How Do I Do It? Important Details

NUMBER OF DAYS (D): This is an easy one to figure but important to future calculations.

NUMBER OF PEOPLE WHO WANT TO EAT (P): Usually everyone wants to eat. Don't trust them if they say they don't. Once they smell your cooking, they'll change their minds.

CALORIC NEEDS AND WEIGHT (W): Some people work these out separately and specifically. We have had a lot of luck generalizing caloric intake and only starved to death once. (We got better later.) If you want to work out your caloric intake specifically, there is a chart in the appendix with the most commonly used backpacking foods and their corresponding calories per pound. There are several software programs available that make this task a breeze.

How Much Food Do I Need?

Food equals weight. And the more energy you exert, the more food you will need. Remember, extreme weather greatly increases your energy output. Below you will find four plans for different types of outdoor adventures. Read them and pick the one that most closely resembles the trip you are currently planning.

PLAN 1: This plan is utilized in very warm conditions when you don't feel superhungry or when activity level is very low. For example: base camps or water trips where you supplement your diet with fishing and/or some fresh and canned food.

Pack 1.5 pounds of food per person per day. Calories will add up to roughly 2,200 to 2,500 per day.

PLAN 2: This is the plan we personally use most often. It keeps most folks content with the food supply on the average backcountry excursion from spring through fall.

Pack between 1.75 and 2.0 pounds of food per person per day. Calculated calories should add up to roughly 2,500 to 3,000 per day.

PLAN 3: This plan works best for folks who are traveling in cold environments or are putting in extremely heavy workdays.

Pack 2.0 to 2.25 pounds of food per person per day. Calculated calories should add up to roughly 3,000 to 3,500 per day.

PLAN 4: This plan is utilized in only the most extreme environments: extreme cold, high-altitude mountaineering, Continental Divide through-hikers, and the like.

Pack 2.5 pounds of food per person per day or more. At this level eating becomes a discipline more than a result of hunger.

Example: two folks are taking a ten-day July backpacking and fishing trip in the Rockies. How much food do they need?

Two people (P) x 10 days (D) x 1.75 lbs. food/day (Plan 2) = 35.0 lbs. of food

These folks need to pack thirty-five pounds of food total for their ten-day trip.

What to Bring: Types of Food

If you are inexperienced with backcountry cooking, we suggest bringing a wide variety of foods and a copy of this book. Then have fun.

We break our rationing down into eight categories and distribute the food as follows:

1. **BREAKFASTS:** About 15 percent of the total weight.
   Examples: Bagels, cream of wheat, Grape-Nuts, granola, hash browns, oatmeal.

2. **DINNERS:** About 20 percent of the total weight.
   Examples: Bulgur, couscous, dried potatoes, falafel, lentils, pasta, instant beans, rice, tortillas.

3. **FLOUR:** About 10 percent of total weight.
   Examples: Wheat, white, cornmeal, baking mix, muffin mix, bread mix.

4. **HIGH-FAT ITEMS:** About 13 percent of total weight.
   Examples: Cheese, margarine, meats, oil, peanut butter.

5. **MUNCHABLES:** About 20 percent of total weight.
   Examples: Candy, crackers, dried fruit, fruit bars, high-energy bars, pita bread, nuts and seeds, trail mix.

6. **DRINKS AND SUGARS:** About 10 percent of total weight.
   Examples: Sugar, fruit crystals, honey, hot chocolate, gelatin.

7. **DESSERTS:** About 3 percent of total weight.
   Examples: Brownie mix, cake mix, cheesecake mix, pudding mix.

8. **MISCELLANEOUS:** About 8 percent of total weight.
   Examples: Milk powder, soup mix, dried vegetables, egg powder,
   tomato base.

Total Ration Planning is not an exact science. If you add up the percentages in the eight categories, you will see that the grand total equals only 99 percent. This gives you a little freedom in packaging and planning. There is a lot of flexibility with the categories, but it is important that your total weight measures up. If you come up light when you weigh your food bag, throw in a couple of your favorite items. If you come up heavy, get rid of something.

The more you use this method, the more you will learn the ins and outs of the foods that will most please you and your companions. If you are having trouble knowing where to begin, Table A will give you a general plan. The table is based on a ten-day ration for two folks, so remember to adjust for number of days times number of people times number of pounds per day to arrive at your grand total of food needed.

Non- or low-caloric items, although you need to bring them along, should not be counted in your total poundage. Examples of these items include: spices, bouillon cubes, hot sauce, coffee, items with NutraSweet, small amounts of dried vegetables, and so on.

Once you become more experienced with Total Ration Planning, feel free to substitute your favorite foods into the plan. But be careful to substitute foods of approximately equal caloric value. For example, if you substitute two pounds of cheese (thirty-two hundred calories) with two pounds of tuna (fourteen hundred), you will end up significantly reducing your total calories by eighteen hundred calories. Additionally, many people decide not to bake. (We can't figure this one out!) Remember, if you're not going to bring flour, you should consider substituting breads and crackers.

Option 2: Specific Menu Planning

Specific Menu Planning works well on short trips (less than a week) or when you have little time or energy to spend on food preparation in the field. Although it is not required, we almost always use this plan for high-altitude or extremely cold-weather trips. It's just so convenient when you crawl into camp exhausted to have a Bag-a-Feast (see Repackaging and Resupplying) ready to go. You don't have to think. This plan also makes more sense for short trips.

How to Do It: Important Details

NUMBER OF SPECIFIC MEALS: How many breakfasts, lunches, and dinners will you need?

TRIP MENU: You will need to decide what you will eat at those specific meals.

NUMBER OF PEOPLE: You will need this to estimate the amount of food needed per meal and some bulk items like drinks, dry milk, oil, and so on. As a starting point, one pound of dry ingredients per meal usually satisfies about three hungry outdoor types.

FINAL CHECK: We get scared because we're used to Total Ration Planning, so, as a final check, we always weigh our food to see if we're in the correct weight range for the number of people times number of days times number of pounds per day.

Sample Menu for a Weekend Trip

FRIDAY	SATURDAY	SUNDAY
	Breakfast	**Breakfast**
	Granola and milk	Pancakes and syrup
	Dried fruit	Dried fruit
	Hot chocolate	International Coffee
	Munchables	**Munchables**
	Cheese and crackers	Meat and crackers
	Fruit bars, gorp	Energy bars and gorp
	Fruit drink	Energy drink
Dinner	**Dinner**	
Tea	Tea	
Curried Rice	Lisagna Lasagna	
Fruit Crunch	Pudding	

Considerations for Special Environments

If you're trying to save weight and water, freeze-dried foods can usually cut 20 percent of your total food poundage and save you significant amounts of fuel as well. This can be very helpful in the desert where water is scarce or in winter when you're melting snow for water.

We never go completely freeze-dried, but we occasionally throw some in for special situations like those listed above or high on mountains when we're almost too tired to breathe, never mind cook. Their light weight also makes them great extra food. Forget them in the bottom of your pack until an emergency arises. It's nice to be able to pull them out and just add hot water.

Table A: Sample Food Ration Plan

10-day ration for 2 people

	1.5 lbs./day per person	1.75 lbs./day per person	2 lbs./day per person	2.25 lbs./day per person
TOTAL	**30 lbs.**	**35 lbs.**	**40 lbs.**	**45 lbs.**
BREAKFASTS				
% OF TOTAL LBS.	**15%**	**15%**	**15%**	**15%**
Bagels	1.0	1.0	2.0	2.0
Cream of wheat		.5	.5	.5
Grape-Nuts	1.0	1.0	1.0	1.0
Granola	.5	.75	.5	1.25
Hash browns	1.0	1.0	1.0	1.0
Oatmeal	1.0	1.0	1.0	1.0
Subtotal	**4.5**	**5.25**	**6.0**	**6.75**
DINNERS				
% OF TOTAL LBS.	**20%**	**20%**	**20%**	**15%**
Bulgur	.5	.5	.5	.5
Couscous			.5	.5
Dried potatoes	.5	.5	1.0	1.0
Falafel	.5	.5		
Lentils		.5	.5	
Macaroni	2.5	2.5	2.5	2.5
Instant potatoes		.5	.5	1.0
Refried beans	.5	.5	.5	.5
Rice	.5	.5	1.0	
Tortillas	1.0	1.0	1.0	1.0
Subtotal	**6.0**	**7.0**	**8.0**	**7.0**
FLOUR				
% OF TOTAL LBS.	**10%**	**10%**	**10%**	**4%**
Basic batter mix	1.5	1.5	1.5	1.0
Cornmeal	.5	.5	.5	
Muffin mix	.5		.5	
Sweet bread mix		.5	.5	
Wheat	.5	.5	1.0	
White	.5	.5		1.0
Subtotal	**3.5**	**3.5**	**4.0**	**2.0**
HIGH-CALORIE, HIGH-FAT ITEMS				
% OF TOTAL LBS.	**13%**	**13%**	**13%**	**18%**
Cheese	2.0	2.0	2.0	3.5
Margarine	1.0	1.0	1.5	2.0
Meats				2.0
Oil	.5	.5	.5	
Peanut butter	.5	1.0	1.0	
Tahini				.5
Subtotal	**4.0**	**4.5**	**5.0**	**8.0**

MUNCHABLES				
% OF TOTAL LBS.	20%	20%	20%	22%
Candy	.5	.5	1.0	1.0
Crackers				.5
Dried fruit	1.5	1.5	1.5	1.0
Fruit bars	1.0	.5	1.0	1.0
High-energy bars	.5	2.0	1.0	2.0
Pita bread				1.0
Nuts and/or seeds	1.5	1.5	1.5	1.5
Trail mix	1.0	1.0	2.0	2.0
Subtotal	**6.0**	**7.0**	**8.0**	**10.0**

DRINKS AND SUGARS				
% OF TOTAL LBS.	10%	10%	10%	12%
Brown sugar	.75	1.0	1.0	1.0
Coffee*				
Fruit crystals (no NutraSweet*)	.5	.75	1.0	1.5
Honey				
Hot chocolate	1.25	1.25	1.5	1.25
Jell-O (no NutraSweet*)		.5	.5	1.25
Tea bags*	20	20	20	20
White sugar				.5
Subtotal	**2.5**	**3.5**	**4.0**	**5.5**

DESSERTS				
% OF TOTAL LBS.	3%	3%	3%	3%
Brownies		.5		.5
Cheesecake			.5	.5
Cake mix	.5	.5	.5	
Pudding	.5	.25	.5	.5
Subtotal	**1.0**	**1.25**	**1.5**	**1.5**

MISCELLANEOUS				
% OF TOTAL LBS.	8%	8%	8%	10%
Bouillon*	yes	yes	yes	yes
Buttermilk		.5	.5	
Cup O Soups	.5	.5	.5	1.0
Dried vegetables*	yes	yes	yes	yes
Egg powder	.5	.5	.5	
Instant soup mix				.5
Milk	1.25	1.25	1.25	1.75
Miso				
Sauce mix*	yes	yes	yes	yes
Ramen soup			.5	.75
Tomato base	.25	.25	.25	.25
Subtotal	**2.5**	**3.0**	**3.5**	**4.25**

* You want to bring items but not count them in your total weight, as they add no or very few calories.

Repackaging and Resupplying

Option 1: Bulk Bagging

Under the Total Ration Plan we package food in one- to two-pound plastic bags without labeling the bags. It is helpful to have a small scale, but, if you don't, there is a pounds-to-cups chart in the appendix with the most commonly packed foods listed.

If you want to label the bags, go ahead, but it's really only necessary for the "white" dry goods. Even with experience, powdered milk, cheesecake, flour, couscous, grits, baking mix, and potato flakes can start to look alike, especially in the dim light of your headlamp.

We prefer two-mil plastic bags that we can tie in a loose knot in the top. This works great, but be prepared to assassinate the first person who carries the bag by the knot. After that the knots are never too tight. Some people prefer to use Ziploc bags, although we find that they often pop open in your pack if you're not careful to remove the air from the bag and keep the food out of the zipper mechanism. It's a good idea to double-bag items such as cheese or margarine (even if they're in screw-top containers) because they can leak oil into your pack. Even bouillon cubes will melt in the heat. You can buy a bag-sealing appliance. They work great, but once you reopen the bag it becomes useless.

If the group size gets much above four or five people, we plan on cooking in two groups. Otherwise the pressure on the stove is too great, and meals start taking longer and longer—which, of course, makes your companions grumpier and grumpier. Three to four people per stove is ideal.

Option 2: Bag-a-Feast

This is more time consuming than bulk bagging, but it will save you a lot of effort in the backcountry. Consult your daily menu and bag all ingredients needed for each individual meal into a single large plastic bag. If all ingredients are not cooked together, small bags may be needed to keep the ingredients separate until you use them. We usually bag breakfasts and dinners, marking them B and D respectively (some people even number them for the specific day), and then have additional bags marked: DRINKS, DESSERTS, SPICES, and OIL/MARGARINE. Munchables are distributed throughout the group.

Sample Bag-a-Feast: Quick Curried Rice

AT HOME: Put rice, bouillon cube, red and green peppers into a half-gallon-sized plastic bag. Put chopped dried fruit, spices, and peppers into a smaller bag and seal. Put nuts and coconut in a smaller bag and seal. Put smaller bags in larger bag and seal.

IN CAMP: Pull out the bag and follow the directions in this book for Quick Curried Rice (see Entrees)

Additional Hints

Most folks can comfortably carry an eight- to ten-day ration of food. After ten days the weight starts cutting into the fun, not to mention your hips.

Some folks like to separate their meals into color-coded or marked bags: breakfast bag, lunch bag, and dinner bag. This works if a group always travels together, but if you don't or you get separated from your party, you may have to eat dry macaroni elbows for lunch. If it's a paddling trip, we advise you to divide the food types between boats. If one boat goes over and you lose a food bag, you won't lose all the candy bars or all the dinner food. These small things can be the key to a happy expedition.

Make sure you pack your stove and fuel well away from and below the food. A fuel leak is a terrible thing to have on top of your food.

Pack several matchbooks (and a lighter) in different places. If you don't, and they rub together and ignite in your pack, you'd better hope somebody on your trip is genetically sound enough to have packed some extra matches.

When repackaging cheese, try not to touch it (wear gloves or plastic bags on your hands). Also, although recycling is a great thing, use fresh bags for cheese. These two things delay mold growth.

Resupplying

For most backcountry trips, after approximately ten days you will have to rendezvous with your resupply or go home.

Whatever method of resupply you choose, make sure the food is packed in weatherproof and animalproof containers. Package your food so the loss of one container doesn't mean the loss of all of one type of food.

Caches

Before the trip begins, you can hide a predetermined amount of food along your route and pick it up later. It's always better if you secure your own cache, since somebody else's X on the map easily turns into a cold, hungry treasure hunt with an unhappy end result. It can be very hard to find caches.

Completely clean up the cache when you're done. Leaving trash and food in the backcountry is uncool.

Caches are illegal in many national parks and designated wilderness areas. Call before you cache.

Roadheads

Plan your trip in a couple of big circles and resupply at your car. Or have a friend meet you at a roadhead with your resupply.

Post Offices

Mail yourself your resupply to a post office along your route. Mail it well in advance with a holding date on the label. Also, many small post offices have limited hours, so be prepared to wait . . . or call first and ask.

Commercial Packers

You can arrange for a commercial packer to deliver your resupply to you at a given place and time. Prices and weight limits vary. If you're using a commercial resupplier, make sure you get everything in writing, including the meeting point and time and what will happen if you're late. Having the resupply dropped indiscriminately means you go hunting for it later. It's not the best plan. The local chamber of commerce closest to the area in which you are traveling can often send you information. Sometimes the National Park Service, U.S. Forest Service, or Bureau of Land Management can be helpful.

Boats and Airplanes

You may be able to arrange resupply by boat if you are traveling past a major watercourse.

We have been resupplied by air several times, but it's not cheap and it is illegal in many places, such as most national parks and designated wilderness areas. The pilots generally prefer to land and hand you your resupply. This should be your first choice, too. Looking for boxes that landed in the trees is no fun, and sometimes they pop open.

Just Add Water: Freeze-Dried and Dehydrated Food

Freeze-dried food has undergone a unique process that goes something like this: The food, cooked or fresh, gets frozen very solid, then placed in freezing temperatures with warm air flowing around it long enough for the moisture to sublimate off. Since ice crystals never form, the cells of the food remain relatively undamaged and most of the nutrition is left intact. More than 99 percent of the food's water is removed, so the result is very light in weight, and the bulk is reduced a little. And since the cells are undamaged, they hydrate quickly and easily.

Dehydrated food is exposed to low heat in order to drive the water out. Old dehydration methods drove out a lot of nutrition as well. Newer methods preserve much of the nutritional value. A dehydrated product has 90 to 97 percent of its water removed. Dehydration shrinks the size of the cells, reducing the weight and bulk a lot, and increasing the time it takes to hydrate the food.

The quality of the hydrated food, whether freeze-dried or dehydrated, depends primarily on its quality before the water was removed. The price of both tends to be high compared to cooking from scratch. Both products offer benefits to the backcountry chef. You can add vegetables and fruits that almost seem fresh to your dishes. You can have a quick, hot meal if you get into camp late. You can combine them with other foods to alter your diet. You can carry a few extra meals in case of an emergency without adding much weight.

Facts and Feelings on Some Dried Foods

(See appendix for ordering information.)

Serving sizes (portions) for freeze-dried/dehydrated meals vary considerably, from three ounces (very small) to fourteen ounces (large). Most people require somewhere around twelve ounces to feel content. Be aware of serving sizes when you buy.

Adventure Foods: Lots of meals, serving sizes for two or four people. Lots of delicious and easy-to-use mixes prepared especially for the BakePacker. Foods come with BakePacker directions and regular directions. They offer a cookbook of recipes for the BakePacker too. A selection of individual food and specialty items, including vegetables and soybean "meatless meats." Some great soups. Available primarily via mail order. Cheesy Tuna Casserole tastes like a good cheesy tuna casserole, but it's better with added cheese. Peanutbutter Bar, very fast to make, is an awesome dessert. Adventure Foods are like real, down-home food. Portions vary from very small to fairly large.

AlpineAire: Very wide variety of no-cooking-required meals, side dishes, soups, and breakfasts. Mostly freeze-dried, some dehydrated. Serving sizes mostly for two people, some meals prepared for four. You can order individual items: meats, rice, pasta, vegetables, cheese powder, tomato powder. Instant (no-cook) rice and pasta are very good. Quick mail-order service. Leonardo da Fettuccine is tasty, but left us still hungry. Wild Tyme Turkey hydrated well, but tasted bland. Overall we found AlpineAire needed lots of added spices to satisfy our taste buds. Portions are medium.

Backpacker's Pantry: Many excellent meals packaged for two or four people. Their full line of outdoor grub includes beverages and snacks (including jerky), breakfasts, vegetarian entrees, meat entrees, side dishes, and desserts. Fast, friendly service. Santa Fe Rice with Chicken is simply the best; Huevos Rancheros is delicious, Asian Fried Rice very good, and Strawberry Cheesecake excellent. We rate Backpacker's Pantry overall best for taste. Portions are medium to large.

Chamy Snacks: They offer more than very tasty, wholesome snacks. Also soups, meats, breads, desserts, and unique meals. Change-of-pace foods such as cranberries and sweet bell peppers, chocolate apricots and wild rice soup. Almond Crusader Bar is a snack-sized fruit cake, delicious. Portions are small to medium.

EcoCuisine: From the garden of Mary Jane Butters, Paradise Farms (Moscow, Idaho), comes this line of certified organically grown foods. They're sold by Ms. Butters as Backcountry Organic and by MSR as EcoCuisine. Breakfasts, dinners, side dishes, breads, and desserts. All vegetarian. Preparation time is longer than other outdoor specialty foods. A little heavier to pack, but, uniquely, all the packaging material is completely burnable. Some truly outstanding tastes. Chocolate Chip Cookies are yummy. The Organic Chilimac was delicious and, even though the package read 2 STANDARD SERVINGS, it went down one throat easily. Portions are medium.

Harvest Foodworks: A choice of eighty meals that serve two. Several desserts, breakfasts, and vegetables are available. No meats or meat products are used. Meals come in reusable, reclosable plastic bags that are marked for measuring up to four cups. Combination of freeze-dried and dehydrated foods taking a bit longer to prepare. Oriental Sweet and Sour Dinner took twenty minutes to cook, but the taste was very good. Their eggs taste like real eggs.

Harvest Foodworks makes wholesome, good-tasting food that we find sometimes needs added spices. Portions are large and filling.

Mountain House: The only truly all-freeze-dried company. Lots of dinners, lunches, breakfasts, desserts, snacks, and vegetables. Currently offer no vegetation entrees. No mail order available, but several mail-order businesses offer Mountain House. Beef Teriyaki hydrated very quickly, tasted good, left us still hungry. Beef Stew hydrated quickly and well, great taste, but we had to eat one each to satisfy our appetites. Nothing disappointed our taste buds. Portions are small to medium.

Outback Oven Foods: Once upon a time these foods bore the name Traveling Light (in fact, that name still appears on the packaging), but the line was purchased by Backpacker's Pantry, improved to be easier to use, and now also bears the name Outback Oven. What you get is gourmet baking at its outdoor finest. Mixes, designed especially for the Outback Oven but usable with any baking method, include fudge brownies rich enough to be candy, carrot cake, breads, quiche, coffee cake, outstanding pizzas, lasagna, chicken potpie—and more. Just like Mama makes it. Mixes fit 8- to 12-inch pans. Portions are large.

Richmoor/Natural High: Richmoor for "camping food" and Natural High for "gourmet camping food." Large selection of dinners (some vegetarian), lunches, and breakfasts that serve two or four. Complete meals are available. Vegetables, desserts, snacks. Combination of freeze-dried and dehydrated. Honey Lime Chicken was a bit sweet, and the chicken didn't quite hydrate in the time they said it would. Chicken Fajitas hydrated easily and well, and the tortilla chips were really crunchy. Thai Beef, with Caramel Vanilla Crème for dessert, provided us an excellent meal. Portions are medium.

Sorrenti Family Farms: Specializes in very tasty fresh-dried wild rice meals in combination with vegetables or fruits, spices, and natural flavorings. No artificial flavorings or preservatives. Ask for the "mini" Quick Gourmet Mixes, packaged for the backcountry. Offers muffin mixes with wild rice flour, and pizza kits. Excellent soups. Wildflower Honey Sticks are a tasty burst of energy. Good wholesome food. Portions small to medium.

Trail Gourmet: All-natural ingredients combined in breakfast and dinner entrees, lunch items, beverages, and snacks (including fat-free Hi-Honey bars). Meals are packaged for either one or two people. Many items available in bulk for those who prefer to prepare their own meals. Easy ordering off the Internet. Preparation time is a bit longer than most, but taste is outstanding. Try the Wild Rice, Blueberries and Yogurt, or Pasta with Chili Pepper Pesto. The pasta melts in your mouth. Portions are large.

High-Energy
Drinks and Bars

The Drinks

t used to be that the experts thought water was absorbed by your body faster than high-energy drinks. Now they say a high-energy drink, one that's up to about 6 percent carbohydrate, is actually absorbed faster than water once it reaches the small intestine. Although plain water and a high-energy drink will have the same influence on body temperature control, metabolic waste removal, and cardiovascular function in general, high-energy drinks provide an energy boost for hardworking muscles. As an added benefit, the drinks give water a sweet taste that encourages consumption. During periods of moderate exercise, you can water down a high-energy drink with three or four times the recommended amount of water.

High-energy drinks also contain electrolytes, particularly sodium, potassium, and chloride, which are necessary to motivate muscles and balance fluids in your body. When you're working hard, some electrolytes, specifically sodium, are lost in your sweat. For most people, a balanced diet replaces all the electrolytes you need. But when the ambient temperature and your exercise level are high, especially when you're not acclimatized to the high heat, you'll benefit from the electrolytes in high-energy drinks.

Salt tablets should be considered a curse, and avoided. They are too strong and can irritate your stomach, cause nausea, and increase your body's need for fluid.

Facts and Feelings on Some High-Energy Drinks

Today's market offers many high-energy drinks. We've used and appreciated these. (See appendix for ordering information.)

E-mergen-C: Energy and electrolytes, plus vitamin C. Handy packets carry one serving. One tangy fruit flavor. Effervescent powder fizzes in your water bottle. If water is low, you can dump the contents straight into your mouth, but be prepared to pucker. We've downed a lot of this one.

Gatorade: The original high-energy drink. Lots of flavors that we like. Six percent carbohydrate. Available as Gatorade Light at 2.5 percent carbohydrate. Available in durable packets that pack well and mix easily. Also available in bulk containers.

Revenge: Twenty grams of carbohydrates in a twenty-nine-gram serving, but the ingredients in this tasty drink, claim the manufacturers, preserve glycogen, deliver more oxygen to starved muscles, and help you utilize stored fats. All we know is that, during heavy exercise, we feel the difference, and it's a good difference.

Sqwincher: This is 6.8 percent carbohydrate in nine fine-tasting flavors. Available in instant dry mix that packs well and mixes easily. Also available in liquid concentrate packets; just add water and drink from the package.

The Bars

Once upon a time, not long ago, there was only PowerBar. Now the market shelves bend under the load of nearly two dozen rivals in the energy bar industry. If you're facing a long day or just want a power-up snack, energy bars can provide a healthy boost. Whatever brand you choose, choose carefully. Energy bars should be no more than 25 percent, or near that, fat. Make sure the bulk of the carbohydrates are complex (rice, oats, glucose polymers, maltodextrin, for example) for staying power, and not simple sugars.

If you're anticipating a long haul, eat a bar before you get going in order to stoke the fires of your engine. If you're pooped at the end of the long haul, eat one to restore your energy. If you need a boost, say every hour or so, take a bite of bar. And remember that energy bars need lots of water to work, so drink regularly and often.

Facts and Feelings on Some Energy Bars

So many energy bars, so little time. And no one seems to feel exactly the same about the same bar. You'll probably want to try several. Then you'll find your favorite, and you'll probably stick with it. We've tried the following, but one of us remains a PowerBar fan, the other a Clif Bar fanatic. (See appendix for ordering information.)

Balance: All Balance Bars are balanced with what they call the 40/30/30 formula: 40 percent carbohydrate, 30 percent protein, 30 percent fat—a complete nutritional food. Added herbs in the Balance+ Bars (such as Honey Peanut with Siberian Ginseng) are supposed to boost energy and clear your mind. Taste is not bad. More than a half dozen "regular" flavors include Banana Coconut and Almond Brownie.

Clif Bar: A beefy dessertlike texture looks tasty and, by golly, it tastes tasty. With a bottle of water, one of these seems like a meal. Bars are now loaded with antioxidants. Low fat. Easy to chew. Eleven flavors, including Chocolate Expresso and Carrot Cake.

Mountain Lift: Nice and chewy, even when the temperature plummets, with herbs added to boost circulation and up the oxygen in your blood. High in protein, low in fat. Taste is very good. Five flavors, including Chocolate and Peanut Crunch.

PowerBar: The bar that made energy bars famous. Taste is very good. The Harvest Line bars are designed as meal replacements with flavors like Blueberry and Strawberry—and they're moist and easy on the teeth. The standard Performance Line includes many flavors, with Malt Nut and Apple Crisp being our favorites. These can be a workout for the jaws, especially if it's cold.

Promax: These hefty bars pack twenty grams of protein in with the usual mix of carbos and fats, vitamins and minerals, producing a hunk of food with smooth texture and okay taste. A half dozen flavors include the fetching titles of Lemon Chiffon and Apple Pie a la Mode.

Tiger Sport: A little on the sweet side and easy to chew, these bars are made by Tiger's Milk, the fitness and bodybuilding people, and taste okay. Low fat. Four flavors.

Setting Up the Outdoor Kitchen

An Environmental Perspective

Within sixty easy paces from one end of the clearing to the other, four old fire rings of blackened rocks surrounding mounds of ash, nearby earth compacted into the consistency of concrete, stand as ugly reminders that camp kitchens may remain to scar the backcountry long after you're history. Not an uncommon sight, but an outdoor kitchen *today* should have as little impact on the environment as possible.

Your environmental kitchen ideally sits in a comfortable spot, protected from unappealing weather conditions, offering an inspiring view. It should also be, ideally, an isolated spot where you aren't an uninspiring view to other backcountry users. And it should be durable, a place that has the best chance to be impacted the least.

The greatest impact of kitchens, and to the backcountry in general, comes from destruction of vegetation and compaction of the soil, with the common result of erosion. Intensity of use determines much of a kitchen's impact (how many people have sat, stood, and walked around there before), but your behavior and your choice of sites will also affect your ability to leave no trace.

Concerning intensity, a heavily used spot—which means a campsite utilized more than ten times, according to the U.S. Forest Service—does not significantly deteriorate with further use. Most of the impact comes in the first one or two times a site is used improperly. That means if you have a choice between an obviously impacted spot and a nearby pristine spot, you'll do far less damage settling where the damage has already been done. But leave it as pretty as possible. In high-use areas you want to encourage other people to use the same site instead of creating a new one.

If you're using an unspoiled spot, choosing the cooking site ranks as the single most important consideration in terms of an environmental kitchen. First, start looking for the best site early, before fatigue or darkness urges you to drop down in the most convenient space. If the site shows evidence of previous use, don't cook there. The ideal spots are without vegetation, or even soil: sand, rocks, gravel, snow. Second best are soil-based sites without vegetation. Even though your stay will cause some compaction, recovery is rapid. If you have to choose between dense vegetation and sparse vegetation, go for the dense. Sparse plant life disturbs easier than a thick carpet of vegetation. Wet grass and dewy flowers die easily when trampled. Low shrubs and baby trees take a long time to come back from abuse. Marshy ground recovers slowly from heavy use. Dense dry grass, on the other hand, or under the other foot, makes a tough, durable surface. An open meadow of grass, even though you'll be more visible to other campers, recovers quicker than thin vegetation hidden under a forest canopy. In short, don't rearrange the earth to suit you, find a spot on it that suits it and you.

Your behavior requires more attention to details. Large parties, groups of more than four or five, leave less impact if they break into smaller kitchen groups. This is especially true in more pristine areas. Wearing soft-soled shoes around the kitchen mars the land less than boots. Reduce your movement around the kitchen as much as possible, especially in vegetated spots. Avoid making trails. Walking back and forth from tent to stove along the same path several times may leave a track noticeable for years. Minimize your stay in one place. It's best for the land if you move every day.

When it's time to move on, check one more time to make sure you're packing out everything you packed in. Look for spillage at the cooking site, flour or rice that puffed out of the pot during mixing, food that fell off the plate during eating in the dark. Fluff up grass or other vegetation that got pressed down. Sprinkle duff or other natural materials over marred areas. Replace rocks or logs you may have rolled out of the way. Use a dead branch to sweep away even your tracks.

Prep Area Versus Cook Area

When you plan a lot of mixing and stirring, establish a food preparation area apart from the cooking area. This will prevent the problem of having to start a pot of water toward boiling a second time because you knocked the first pot over.

Safe Food Storage

Improper storage of camp food can attract unwelcome visitors: the small ones that might eat your food, and the big ones that might eat you. Since your cooking area will be well away from your sleeping area, keeping all food in the cooking area concentrates odors in one relatively safe spot. We carry food double-bagged in plastic in a zippered duffel bag to reduce odor even more. Odorous garbage stays in the food storage bag, in its own separate bag. If the chance of a bear encounter is minimal, you can leave the food on the ground or, preferably, hang it casually from the limb of a tree. If bears frequent the area, better hang the food high. The most bearproof hanging method requires the food bag be suspended between two trees, a minimum of 12 feet off the ground and a minimum of 12 feet from each tree. This is a laborious process, but we've used it where bear populations are dense. You can usually get by hauling the food bag up about 12 feet off the ground from a limb. A new contraption, an unbreakable bearproof plastic container, guarantees that your food will be safe. It might be worth the money and weight if bears are thick and trees are not.

Quick Summary

1. Minimize environmental damage.
2. Minimize visual contact with other folks.
3. Maximize protection from unwelcome weather.
4. Maximize protection from unwelcome pests.
5. Maximize view.

Stoves and Fuel

Beneath every delicious one-burner meal you'll find, at some point, a one-burner stove. Your choice of stoves will help determine the outcome of meal preparation . . . and your level of frustration during cooking. Although you may not find one ideal stove for all occasions, these general tips should help you make your choice.

1. **Weight and size:** Some excellent stoves weigh far too much and take up too much room to be practical in the wilderness. Happy cooks choose a stove that packs easily and weighs in between a pound and a pound and a half when empty of fuel.

2. **Heat output intensity and range:** The more intense the heat, measured in BTUs, the less time it takes to boil water. Efficient stoves will boil a quart of water in less than five minutes. But intense heat is not something you'll want all the time. Chefs need to be able to turn the heat down in order to simmer some fine meals.

3. **Ease of operation:** A stove that starts easily and handles easily, even in cold weather, is the stove you want.

4. **Stability:** Stoves that wobble when you set a pot on the burner are likely to dump your well-earned gourmet meal in the dirt. Choose a stove with a stable base, one that has an adequate pot-supporting surface and a relatively low profile.

5. **Windscreens:** Wind reduces the efficiency of your stove. Wind can snuff out the flame when you need it most. You can't control the wind, but you can choose a stove with a windscreen . . . or one for which you can make a windscreen.

6. **Durability:** Packs with stoves stuffed inside get dropped, sat on, stuffed into trunks of cars, and banged against trees. Choose a stove that can withstand the punishment.

7. **Accessories:** Some stoves come with a fuel bottle. That's nice. Some stoves come with a stuff sack. That's nice, too . . . protective sacks add to the life expectancy of your stove. Some stoves come with repair kits. Another nice option. You don't want to be far from home without a stove repair kit.

8. **Fuel used:** In the United States any fuel you want is available. In many foreign countries fuel types are limited. Make sure your stove will utilize the fuel you'll have available.

9. Cost: The amount you pay does not necessarily indicate the efficiency of the stove for your purposes. Choose the stove that will work best, and then decide how to pay for it.

Stove Fuels

- **Alcohol:** Heat output is low. Flammability is high. Burns clean, and spills evaporate quickly without leaving a harmful residue.

- **Automotive gasoline:** Use unleaded only; leaded gas produces toxic fumes when burned. Explosions are possible. Heat output is high. Flammability is also high. Stoves may clog with prolonged use.

- **Butane:** Must be carried in cartridges. Burns clean. Most cartridges can't be changed until they're empty, and heat output goes down as fuel runs low. Easy and safe to use. Heat output is reduced by cold temperatures. Must be kept above freezing.

- **Butane/propane mix:** Must be carried in cartridges. Burns clean. Easy and safe to use. Performs well at high altitude and in cold temperatures.

- **Kerosene:** Heat output high. Flammability lowest of all fuels, but it smells. If you spill, some it remains oily—unlike other fuels, which evaporate quickly.

- **Propane:** Must be carried in cartridges. Burns clean. Easy and safe to use. Performs well in cold.

- **White gas (or naphtha):** Heat output is high. Flammability is high, and explosions are possible. Burns clean. Much cheaper than cartridges of fuel. Works well at high altitude. Works well in cold although preheating burner might be required.

Tips for Figuring Liquid Fuel Needs

- On summer trips figure one sixth of a quart per person per day. That's three sixths or a half quart per person for a three-day trip; one quart per person for a six-day trip.

- On fall and spring trips figure a quarter quart per person per day, especially if you're traveling in a cold climate and/or at higher altitudes.

- On winter trips and at high altitude, figure a half quart per person per day, especially if you're melting snow for water. Better safe than sorry.

Stove Safety and Maintenance Tips

1. Keep your stove covered when you're not using it. Carry it in a stuff sack or kit. Keeping dirt and dust out of your stove prolongs its life and reduces maintenance.

2. Be sure your gas stove is cool before refilling. Refill outside your tent and well away from other heat sources. Use a funnel or a fuel bottle cap with a built-in pour spout to avoid spillage when refueling.

3. Fill stoves and fuel bottles that attach to stoves no more than two thirds to three quarters full in order to maintain air space for pressure.

4. If fuel spills on the stove during filling, allow it to evaporate before lighting.

5. If you melt snow for water, plan on at least two quarts per person per week.

6. Using a cover on pots while cooking reduces the amount of fuel you'll use.

7. Carry and store stoves and fuel well separated from foods.

8. Carry fuel in containers made for carrying fuel.

9. Do not burn automotive gasoline in a tent or snow cave or any enclosed area. If you must cook inside a tent or snow cave with fuel other than auto gas, light the stove outside the enclosed area, then move it inside. Make sure adequate ventilation is maintained at all times.

10. Try new stoves in your backyard before heading out on the long trail.

11. Practice taking your stove apart at home in case you have to repair it in the field.

12. Carry a stove repair kit.

Facts and Feelings on Some Stoves

(See appendix for ordering information.)

Bibler

Hanging Stove: Innovative, this stove hangs from anything convenient, including the inside of your tent, if you're careful and provide adequate ventilation. Weighs in at twenty-nine ounces, which includes the two-quart pot, lid, and handle. Great stability when hanging. Windscreen/heat reflector envelops the pot and burner for efficiency. Easy to use. Requires a butane/propane cartridge.

Camping Gaz

Rando 360: Very compact. Comes with two pots, windscreen, pot clamp, and strap that nest together tidily. Weight without cartridge twenty-two ounces. Low profile makes stability good. Uses a butane cartridge that burns about one hour at full strength. Takes longer than many stoves to boil a quart of water. Not good for group cooking.

Some packing stoves

Peak 1

Ultra 470

MSR XGK

Ultra 470: Supersized butane/propane cartridge burns about four and a half hour. Stove screws into top of cartridge. Boils a quart of water in under five minutes. Weight with cartridge forty-one ounces. Automatic ignition. Stable when base ring is used.

Coleman

The Coleman Company, long a leader in outdoor stoves, has several excellent one-burners; (and one two-burner), including:

Peak 1 Apex and Apex II: Pump fits into fuel bottle, connected to stove via a flexible hose. Weighs in at 18.6 ounces. High heat output with great simmering ability. Easy to use. Low profile for stability. Apex uses white gas, Apex II uses white gas or unleaded gasoline. Both are adaptable to kerosene.

Peak 1 Feather 442 Dual Fuel: One-piece stove. Weighs 23.25 ounces. High heat output, simmers great. Easy to use. Fold-out legs provide good stability. Packs neatly in padded stuff sack (sold separately). Windscreen available. Uses white gas or unleaded gasoline. One of our favorites.

Peak 1 Multi-Fuel: Like a smaller Feather 442. Weighs 20.8 ounces. High heat output, simmers just fine. Easy to use. Burns white gas or adapts to kerosene.

Powermax: A series of three light and fast stoves: Xtreme at eleven ounces, Xpert at fourteen ounces, and the one-of-a-kind backpacking two-burner Xpedition at twenty-five ounces. All fold up neatly into tidy little bags for easy packing. They plug into a fuel bottle and burn white gas. High-intensity heat. Efficient. Very stable.

Mountain Safety Research

XGK Expedition: It's been around a long time, and it's proven its worth. Burns almost any fuel. When the temperature plunges and the altitude soars, the XGK delivers high heat. No one-burner boils water faster. Excellent for mountaineering. Fairly easy to use. Priming required. Pump fits in fuel bottle and connects to stove via rigid tube. Kind of awkward to pack safely, and a bit tippy on rough terrain. Noisy. Does not simmer. Weighs in at 15.5 ounces with fuel pump, windscreen, heat reflector, and stuff sack. Our favorite at high altitude.

WhisperLite: Easy to use, works well in cold . . . and quiet, as the name implies. Produces intense heat but adjusts to simmer a meal as well. Folds up to pack neatly inside many pots. More stable than the XGK. Burns white gas only. Weighs in at 13.5 ounces with fuel pump, windscreen, heat reflector, and stuff sack.

WhisperLite Internationale: Very much like the WhisperLite, but it also burns kerosene. Same weight, same accessories.

DragonFly: Easy to use and burns just about anything for fuel. Folds up for easy packing. Very stable with a pot on top. Fully adjustable flame, from low simmer to rapid boil, makes this an excellent choice for the backcountry gourmet. Weighs 17.1 ounces.

SuperFly: A butane-burning stove that fits most butane cartridges. Fairly stable on the ground. Very stable in the air, which is possible with an optional hanging system. Easy to use. Stove weighs in at a tiny 4.5 ounces.

RapidFire: Simple to use. Variable flame control. Burns isobutane fuel from cartridge. Cartridge may be removed from stove for easier packing. Weight with windscreen, heat reflector, and stuff sack 12.5 ounces.

Optimus

Optimus 111 Hiker: Stable, must be primed, works well in wind and cold. Unit folds up into heavy but very durable 7- by 7-inch box. Weighs in at fifty-four ounces. Adjustable intensity, with great simmering ability. Burns white gas, kerosene, or alcohol. A proven performer in the arena of one-burners. One of our favorites.

Optimus 123R Climber (Svea): Compact and durable, a bit tippy, works well at higher altitudes but performs less well in cold. Must be primed. Burns white gas only. Loses efficiency without windscreen. Weighs in at 19.5 ounces.

Primus

Primus 2243: Made in Sweden, Primus stoves use a butane/propane cartridge. Heat output is high, and flame is easily adjusted. Built-in wind baffle for more efficiency. Packs easily. Fairly stable with addition of cartridge support. Additional Power Booster transfers heat from burner to cartridge for more efficiency in cold. Automatic ignition available. Appliance weighs about nine ounces.

Primus 2263: Similar to 2243 but less efficient. No wind baffle. Appliance weight about 4.5 ounces.

Primus 3263: Similar to 2263 but comes with automatic ignition. Appliance weight about seven ounces.

Primus 3233: Stable spiderlike stove with cartridge attached by hose. Heat output high. Packs small. Automatic ignition. Appliance weighs about thirteen ounces.

Your Stove in the Cold Outdoors

When it gets really cold, neither you nor your stove is going to function optimally. Some stoves will require preheating. Some stoves won't work at all, especially some of the cartridge types. If you plan to cook outside in winter conditions, make sure you know your stove's capabilities.

Your Stove at High Altitude

When you go up in altitude, the amount of oxygen you and your stove take in with each breath goes down. At 18,000 feet the oxygen in the ambient air is only about half what it is at sea level. That means the efficiency of your stove goes down. If there's not enough oxygen for your stove to burn all the fuel being released, the flame will be cooler and yellower. If you plan to go high, make sure you know your stove's capabilities.

And remember, water boils at a lower temperature the higher you go. That adds to inefficiency, also. So it takes longer to cook food at altitude, which means you'll need more fuel. Plan accordingly.

Gear for the
Outdoor Kitchen

As every cook and carpenter knows, one of the big secrets of a great product is using the right tool for the job. In the backcountry gourmet meals can be prepared with a minimum of simple cook gear, but it should be thoughtfully chosen for maximum chef-ness. (See appendix for ordering information.)

Pots and Pans

Stainless steel pots cost more and weigh a little more, but they hold up better under outdoor abuse, and they're a bit easier to clean. They conduct heat a little slower than aluminum. Some outdoor stainless steel pots have copper on the bottom to increase heat conductivity. We prefer stainless steel.

We've read those stories about how **aluminum** flakes off into food, but not enough would ever flake off your outdoor pots to cause a health problem. For those bored with the dull gray of standard pots and pans, a couple of manufacturers offer aluminum cookware coated with a heat-sealed color, such as dark green (Evolution from Backpacker's Pantry) or black (BlackLite from MSR). It's a nice touch, but the real niceness is the nonstick coating on the inside and the lighter-than-ever weight. Aluminum is a good choice: it's light, it's inexpensive, it's available, it works.

Then there is **titanium,** high-tech metal with a greater strength-to-weight ratio than any other outdoor cookware. If you're the kind of cook who'll cut the handles off spoons to save weight, 1) you're silly, and 2) you'll love titanium. *Beware:* It does not heat as evenly as stainless steel or aluminum, the thin walls dent easier, and it definitely costs the most.

Enamel cookware, although functional and colorful, chips and rusts too easily for us. It is quite safe to use outdoors, the metals under enamel being inert, which means they won't affect your health if you swallow some.

Nonstick coatings, such as Teflon, on pots and pans are also made from inert materials. If you choose a nonstick coating for your outdoor cookware, don't worry about chips and don't worry about the coating when it rubs off in spots. Chips will pass harmlessly through your digestive tract, if you swallow one, and there's no health reason to discard pots and pans with worn surfaces.

Depending on the length of trip and number of people, you'll probably want to own a set of pots ranging in size from one to four quarts. You'll decide what you need and carry those pots you'll need to do the job for a particular trip. Even when it's just the two of us, we carry two pots: one to boil water and one to cook in, or one to mix in and one to cook in. Buy sets that nest together for packability. Some people prefer pots with handles, but we find the handles get so hot that we end up using pot grips anyway. It is important that all pots have a lid that fits well. Lids make cooking faster, hold in heat while you're waiting, and reduce the amount of pine needles and grit in your food. Make sure you choose pots with a very limited number of plastic parts.

One pan approximately 10 inches in diameter, the deeper the better (say 2 inches), with a nonstick surface is a must for fine cooking. Choose one with a lid. Once again, some people like pans with a folding handle, but we use pot grips for a handleless pan, too. Our favorite is the Banks Fry-Bake pan, an aluminum pan with an anodized hard coat for easy cleaning and great durability. It comes in two sizes: the 10.5-inch-diameter Expedition, perfect for a meal for two, and the 8-inch diameter Alpine, intended for one, but you can crowd in enough for two. The snug-fitting lid allows you to build a twiggy fire on top if baking requires one. It is available only via mail order.

Pressure cookers can cut cooking time for things like beans almost in half. For high-altitude trips, you'll save lots of time and fuel. We don't know of a source of pressure cookers designed especially for outdoor use. Small models are available but very hard to find.

Coffee percolators just right for one-burner stoves and mini espresso markers are even available from several manufacturers. Coffee connoisseurs will want the extra weight and bulk, but good old "cowboy coffee" can still be made in any pot.

Outback Oven

For easy, high-quality baking on a one-burner stove, nothing beats the Outback Oven from Backpacker's Pantry. It's not totally foolproof, but a little practice and you'll turn out fabulous breads, pizza, and desserts. The Outback Oven Ultralight in-cludes a diffuser plate and riser bars to create hot air out of your stove's energy, a fabric convection dome to trap the hot air around your personal pan or pot, and a thermometer to monitor baking temperatures. The Outback Oven Plus Eight includes, in addition to the oven system, an 8-inch coated pan with lid; the Plus Ten increases the pan size to 10 inches. The Outback Oven Outfitter includes a 12-inch pan plus a pot lifter, spatula-knife, and cutting board. The accessories are also sold separately. Backpacker's Pantry offers a line of food mixes prepared especially for the Outback Oven.

BakePacker

For the ultimate in simple baking, try the BakePacker from Strike 2 Industries. You just put mixed ingredients in a plastic (yes, plastic) bag, place the bag in your pot on top of the BakePacker, make sure enough water has been added to the pot to cover the cells of the oven, and boil. Because the food is steam-baked, you don't get crusty tops, but the system works, and messy postbaking cleanup is eliminated. Adventure Foods sells mixes prepared especially for the Bake-Packer.

Kitchen Accessories

You'll probably be sorry if you don't have a large spoon to serve and stir with, and a spatula. Pot grips are useful, but we carry a small survival tool (Leatherman) that has pliers that work as pot grips, a knife, can opener, and other often-handy attachments. You'll need some plastic containers in various sizes for things such as butter or cooking oil, and spices. Be warned that the Environmental Protection Agency (EPA) advises not using 35mm plastic film canisters for foodstuffs, since the plasticizers may rub off into your food. Leftover plastic containers that once contained butter or the like do work, but they sometimes pop open in your pack. We generally prefer containers with screw-on tops. (*Hint:* If you have small spice/salt/pepper containers with screw-on tops, measure how much the top holds in order to use that measurement later.) Optional items include a small wire whisk, a measuring cup, an abrasive pad for cleanup, and large collapsible water container to keep water readily available in the kitchen.

Much of the frenetic bother of searching for smaller kitchen items can be eliminated by purchasing one of several kitchen-organizer kits. Atwater Carey, Ltd., offers the Campside Kitchen with two (each) Lexan knives, forks, and spoons, plus a serving spoon, whisk, can opener, spatula, scrubber, collapsible paper measuring cup, and nine containers of various sizes for spices and such. Mesh pockets with lots of room let you carry personal additions. We prefer the Campside Jr.—a smaller version with ample room for gear for two. Outdoor Research Kitchen Kits offer the same conveniences in four sizes: Solo, Hiker (perfect for two), Backpacker, and Camper.

Personal Items

Everyone needs their personal mug, and we prefer the plastic insulated travel variety, twelve to sixteen ounces, with snap-on lid. Drinks in metal cups seem to always be too hot or too cold. When you know the capacity, they can be used as guestimators for measuring. To reduce the guesswork, mark your travel mug before your trip. You see these mugs for sale everywhere. Your personal water bottle can be purchased with measuring grids premarked by the manufacturer.

A personal bowl is needed when a group travels together. When it's just the two of us, we often eat out of the pots and pans. An unbreakable plastic spoon is needed for eating . . . unless you want to carve some chopsticks, which we've done when somehow the spoons got left at home. (*Hint:* If you measure your spoon to see how much it holds, you might find that measurement useful later.) We've never found a need for forks.

Our Personal Outdoor Kitchen Gear Checklist

- ☐ Personal cup
- ☐ Personal bowl
- ☐ Personal spoon
- ☐ Leatherman (for knife, pot grips, can opener)
- ☐ One-quart and two-quart pots with lids
- ☐ Banks Fry-Bake pan with lid
- ☐ Large collapsible water container
- ☐ Atwater Carey Campside Jr. (with small containers, spatula, large spoon, wire whisk, scrubbing pad)
- ☐ Backpacker's Pantry's large convection dome (made for the Outback Oven)

Camp Kitchen Hygiene

A Clean Kitchen Is a Healthy Kitchen

Germs (bacteria, viruses, parasites) are responsible for illnesses (including yucky stomachs) and the early retirement of more backcountry chefs than all other reasons combined. Many germs commonly lurk in backcountry water. Others proliferate in food that's been improperly cooked or stored.

Some germs live long, happy lives on human skin, even healthy humans, without bothering those people. But when some of those same germs fall off into breakfast, lunch, or dinner preparations, they multiply with great speed and lead to disease. Unhealthy people carry germs that can often be passed easily by hand and mouth. And—disgusting but true—humans have germs living in their bowels, and they share those germs in the camp kitchen when they fail to adequately wash their hands after a bowel movement.

Hand Washing

All good cooks have at least one thing in common: clean hands. Your outer layer of skin is an overlapping armor of dead cells that protect the living cells beneath. Under a microscope this outer layer looks like the surface of the Colorado Plateau from 30,000 feet: canyons and mesas, cracks and fissures. Resident microbes are wedged firmly into the low spots. Some of these microbes are friendly, serving to keep skin slightly acid and resistant to other microbial lifeforms such as fungi. Others can make you severely sick. In addition to the residents, transient germs come and go as fortune dictates. They can accumulate rapidly after bowel movements, and they congregate most thickly under fingernails and in the deeper fissures of fingertips. That's why human hands account for 25 to 40 percent of all foodborne illness.

Hand washing prior to food handling, even with detergents, does not remove all the flora, but it does significantly reduce the chance of contamination. For your information, science recommends the following eight-step hand-washing technique for maximum cleanliness:

1. Wet hands with hot flowing water (100 to 120 degrees F).

2. Soap up until a good lather is attained.

3. Work the lather all over the surface of the hand, concentrating on fingernails and tips.

4. Clean under fingernails.

5. Rinse thoroughly with hot water (very important).

6. Resoap and relather.

7. Rerinse.

8. Dry with a paper towel (very important) to wipe off bacteria clinging to the water.

For most of us, hot water is a rare wilderness commodity. But you can still get clean hands with this modified backcountry technique, which substitutes germicidal soap for hot water. In tests, adequate hand sanitation was achieved with as little as a half liter of water. Move at least 200 feet away (seventy adult paces) from the source of water when using any soap in the wilderness.

1. Wet hands thoroughly.

2. Add a small amount of germicidal soap (such as Klenzade, Betadine Scrub, or Hibiclens).

3. Work lather up, especially fingertips.

4. Clean under fingernails (and keep your nails trimmed).

5. Rinse thoroughly.

6. Repeat soap, lather, and rinse.

7. Dry with a small clean towel or bandanna.

In a rush? Join the crowd, but not the sick crowd. Some products provide quick hand sanitization with a fast but thorough rub-and-let-dry. They work, but they are made with alcohol or other rather potent chemicals that can be harsh to your skin with constant use. We've used and liked Hand Sanitizer from Atwater Carey, Ltd., which has moisturizers added to help counter the drying qualities of its germ-killing agent. And we recommend a good hand washing with soap and water at least once a day even if you're using the quick fix of chemicals.

Food Handling

Wilderness food usually shows up in plastic bags, and food contamination can be further reduced by pouring the food out instead of reaching in for it. It ought to go without saying, but here it is anyway: Already-sick people should stay out of the kitchen.

Some well-cooked backcountry food doesn't get the opportunity to be processed by the human digestive system. This results from cooking more than you can eat, which is a result, most often, of less-than-maximal meal-planning skills. Storage of cooked-but-uneaten food in the wilderness poses an almost unsurmountable problem. Bacteria grows optimally at temperatures ranging from 45 to 90 degrees F, and unhealthy populations of bacteria can be reached in a brief period of time. A tuna sandwich on a warm day can become dangerous in less than four hours. Reheating cooked food, although it kills bacteria, often leaves dangerous toxins produced by the bacteria at sickening levels. Your safest bet is not to eat leftovers.

Food waiting to be cooked and waiting to be eaten should be covered in the presence of flies and other germ-toting creatures of the air and ground. Food should be stored out of reach of those same creatures.

Cook Gear and Kitchen Utensils

Another major source of food contamination in the wilderness is dirty cookware and kitchen utensils. Your choice of cookware, say aluminum versus stainless steel, and utensils, say wood versus plastic, is irrelevant in terms of germs, but cookware should be washed and dried daily, and utensils should be cleaned prior to use in the preparation and serving of food. An exception would be extremely cold conditions in which food residue freezes before you can wash it off.

Pack It In, Pack It Out

As any sanitation engineer can tell you, much can be learned about people by going through their garbage. Same goes for backcountry trash and, in the plus column, the amount of litter has steadily decreased in wilderness areas over the last twenty years despite an increase in litter bearers. But the potential impact of trash ranks low as a health hazard, while the disposition of leftover food and, far more important, human waste products ranks as the greatest risk.

What to Do With Your Doo

You can't realistically pack out everything you pack in, except in special circumstances (such as dragging frozen feces off winter trips), but you can, with an adequate poo-poo plan, reduce the risk of fecal contamination to an absolute minimum. Transmission of fecalborne pathogens occurs in four ways: direct contact with the feces (even using toilet paper leaves germs on your hands), indirect contact with hands that have directly contacted the feces, contact with insects that have contacted the feces, and drinking water contaminated with feces.

Human waste products break down to a harmless state as a result of two mechanisms: 1) bacterial action in the presence of oxygen, moisture, and warmth, and 2) inactivation from direct ultraviolet radiation and dryness. Deposition of solid body wastes should include placement to maximize decomposition, to minimize the chance of something or someone finding it, and to minimize the chance of water contamination. And after the deed, wash your hands.

Latrines are out, except in established spots. They concentrate too much poop in one place. They carry a high risk of water pollution. They invite insect and mammal investigation. They are unsightly, and they stink. If you are ever required to dig a latrine, make it at least a foot deep, add soil after each deposit, and fill it in when the total excreta lies several inches below the surface.

For years, environment- and health-concerned wildland managers have recommended catholes as the best way to manage human feces. Preferably in a level spot, a cathole should be dug several inches into an organic layer of soil, where decomposing microorganisms live most abundantly. After you've dropped your droppings, stir them into the soil to speed decomposition. Cover the mess with a couple of inches of soil, and disguise the spot to hide it from later passersby.

Although urine contains, normally, an insignificant number of bacteria, it can carry, almost always in developing countries, parasites such as schistosomes. To stay on the safe side, urinate on rocks or in nonvegetated spots far from water sources and your kitchen whenever possible . . . unless otherwise directed by a wildland manager, who may ask you to pee in a river or lake. Urine on the rocks keeps animals from creating an unsightly excavation later.

Care, But Don't Always Share

Nice people are willing to share, but they may be passing around more than their water bottle. Keep your lip balm and your toothbrush to yourself. Personal eating utensils and mugs should stay personal. If you can't finish your candy bar or your lunch, dispose of the leftovers properly instead of passing your germs to someone else.

Water Disinfection

Many invisible bacteria, viruses, and parasites find a home in water, and all wilderness water sources should be eyed with suspicion in relation to health. It's not the visible stuff in water that makes you sick, but water with a lot of sediment in it should be strained. You can strain it through anything that will let water pass while trapping the sediment: bandanna, T-shirt, paper coffee filter. But good camp kitchen hygiene requires safe water, and there are still, basically, three ways to ensure the quality of water.

Heat

Killing all the microorganisms in water, a process known as sterilization, requires five to ten minutes of boiling at sea level. But not all microorganisms cause illness. Take heat-resistant bacterial spores. They're harmless. Pasteurization, the process of bringing a liquid to almost boiling, works toward killing everything in water that can make a human sick. *Giardia* dies in two to three minutes at 158 degrees F. Viruses die in seconds at 176 degrees F. By the time water reaches the boiling point, worldwide, it's safe to drink, even at an altitude of 19,000 feet, where the boiling point of water is 178 degrees F. Water used to cook with does not have to be disinfected prior to use. The cooking process will disinfect it.

Halogenation

Iodine and chlorine are the best chemical water disinfectants. When used properly, they'll kill most parasites, viruses, and bacteria. They have not, however, been proven effective against Cryptosporidia. The effectiveness of halogens depends on their concentration in the water and the amount of time you wait before drinking. In other words, you can reduce the amount of halogen if you're willing to wait longer for it to work. Cold water slows the effect of chemical disinfectants. In cold water you should use more or wait longer. When opting for halogen use, the safest approach is buying a commercial product and following the instructions. If you're carrying chemical disinfectants, use them in all your drinking water and wait until they have acted before adding anything to the water to sweeten or flavor it.

Filtration

Many backcountry water filters remove protozoan lifeforms and bacteria, but none will remove viruses. Some filters kill viruses via contact with an iodine resin on the filter. Read the label carefully before buying. Most wilderness water in the United States stands or runs free of harmful viruses. Not so in many foreign countries. If you're carrying a filter, use it to disinfect all drinking water before consumption.

Facts and Feelings on Some Water Filters

(See appendix for ordering information.)

First Need Deluxe Purifier: A trademarked "structured matrix" filter. Fairly lightweight, good quality, relatively easy to use. Prefilter strains out large debris; filter eliminates protozoans, bacteria, and viruses without chemicals. Also removes chemical contaminants, bad tastes, and nasty odors. Can be cleaned in the field. EPA approved as a water purifier. Reasonably priced. Highly recommended.

Katadyn Pocket Filter: Ceramic filter. Dependable, durable, precisely manufactured Swiss product, the look and feel of a fine tool. Prefilter strains out large debris. Filter strains out parasites and bacteria. Does not strain out viruses, chemical pollutants, bad tastes, and offensive odors. Pumping requires a lot of effort. Requires frequent cleaning, but can be cleaned easily in the field. Very expensive. Katadyn's Mini Filter is a smaller version.

MSR WaterWorks II: Carbon block plus membrane filter. Innovative, high quality. Prefilter strains out large debris. Parasites and bacteria are strained out. Viruses can get through. Carbon absorbs chemicals and particles that smell or taste bad. Long lever makes it easy to pump. Can be cleaned in the field, but it's a complex process. MSR MiniWorks is a smaller, less effective filter. Fairly expensive.

PUR Explorer: Membrane with iodine resin filter. Truly innovative, high quality. Prefilter strains out big stuff. Filter strains out parasites and bacteria. Iodine resin kills viruses. Add-on carbon filter removes tastes and smells. Easy to use. Easy to clean in the field. Fairly expensive. PUR's Scout and Voyageur, less expensive filters, are also highly recommended—and all three of these PUR products are EPA approved as water purifiers.

SweetWater Guardian: Stainless steel screen and depth filter. A step forward in innovation. Prefilter for the big chunks. Screen and depth filter keep out parasites and bacteria. Lightweight, easy to clean. Easiest of all to pump. Relatively inexpensive. Highly recommended.

First Need · MSR · SweetWater · PUR Explorer · PUR Scout · Katadyn Mini · Katadyn Pocket

Quick Summary

1. Keep your hands clean.
2. Don't save leftovers overnight.
3. Wash and dry your cook gear and personal utensils daily.
4. Pack it in, pack it out.
5. Have a hygienic poo-poo plan.
6. Don't share too much.
7. Disinfect all water.

Cooking Tips and Other Bits of Friendly Advice

Spice Up Your Life

The spice kit is the backcountry chef's best friend. We bring an extensive spice kit when using the Total Food Rationing plan, and a limited one even when we're carrying primarily prepackaged foods.

The spice kit is the easiest way to make a good friend or a worst enemy. Remember to add spices a little bit at a time. Some spices, like the peppers, increase in strength as they cook, so wait a while between dashes. (A dash is less than a pinch. A pinch is about an eighth of a teaspoon). It's relatively easy to go from cardboard flavor to red-hot chili pepper fire if you're not paying attention.

Use a spoon or a shaker lid to add your spices to food. A whole canister of accidental curry is hard to choke down (even on potatoes). And your hands are dirty utensils. Take heed: Rubbing your eye with cayenne is no fun.

If worse comes to worst, spices can be added to individual portions, which is especially useful if you have a companion who has had his "hot" buds surgically removed.

Don't carry your spices in film canisters. Yes, it's a handy size, but they're not safe for food unless you like eating plastic. Many small canisters are commercially available (some are even sold with the spices in them!), or you can use baby bottle bags and tie a *loose* knot in the top. Label your spices if you want.

Once they're individually packaged, carry all your spices together in a single bag: your spice kit.

Popular Spices and Their Common Uses

SALT: White granules. Tastes like salt! Salt is added into almost all recipes but is not a required ingredient. If your food tastes bland or "soapy," it's probably because you need a little salt. Salt brings out the flavor. Remember: Instant soups, bouillon, soy, and tamari all contain salt, as do most prepackaged meals. Salt is not a "bad" thing nutritionally; in fact, you need salt to function healthily. Too much salt is sometimes a problem for folks who have hypertension.

BAKING POWDER: Buy double-acting. This is a white powder that is used as a leavening agent in quick breads, cakes, and biscuits.

BAKING YEAST: Light brown granules used in yeast bread recipes.

BASIL: Dark green, chopped leaves that smell sweet. Great in tomato and cream sauces. We use this a lot on pasta, pizzas, and potatoes.

BLACK PEPPER: Looks like ground-up rock. We put this on almost every dish we make.

CAYENNE: Ground red pepper. Neon red powder that is very hot. Be careful.

CHILI PEPPER: Deep red granules. Spicy; used mostly in Mexican dishes.

CINNAMON: Fine brown powder with a strong sweet smell. Great in porridge, sweet breads, cobblers, and cakes.

CRUSHED RED PEPPER: Red flakes with bits of yellow. Very hot. Use with caution.

CUMIN POWDER: Greenish brown powder used in many Mexican dishes. Especially good on beans. This spice is commonly confused with curry powder.

CURRY POWDER: A gold powder with a strong smell and taste. Can be hot and spicy if you use enough. Food turns gold when you sprinkle it on. (At that point it's too late to turn back.) Used commonly in rice and fruit dishes.

DILL WEED: Looks like chopped thin grass. Smells like a sweet perfume. Good in creamy soups and sauces and breads.

GARLIC POWDER: Pale yellowish white granules. Smells like garlic! Adds flavor to almost all of our dishes and keeps vampires away; an eighth of a teaspoon equals about one clove of fresh garlic.

MRS. DASH: Comes commercially in a variety of mixes. Great on fish or any casserole to perk it up quickly. Lemon and garlic flavors are particular hits.

MUSTARD: Bright yellow powder. Tastes like a hot mustard. Good in cream sauces, pasta, and bean dishes.

ONION FLAKES: Hard white flakes that smell like onion. These need to be hydrated to be used for their best potential. One tablespoon equals about half a medium onion.

OREGANO: Light green leaf bits. Smells strong. Great in Italian dishes. Often mistaken for basil, but they interchange so nicely it really doesn't matter.

PARSLEY FLAKES: Greenish leafy bits. Good in pasta or grain dishes or sprinkled on fish.

Condiments

HOT SAUCES: These come in a variety of brands. Pick your favorite and bring a small plastic bottle along, especially on extended journeys.

SOY SAUCE OR TAMARI: Salty, dark liquid. Great in soups and sauces, over grains, and lentils. Good on popcorn. Can be purchased in a powdered form.

VANILLA EXTRACT: A brown liquid that smells sweet. Useful in baking and frostings. Nice addition to hot cereals and hot drinks.

VINEGAR: Clear or wine-colored, tangy liquid. We usually bring clear for its broader application. Useful in sweet-and-sour, salsa, and peanut butter sauces.

Thickening Agents

Utilizing the crude measuring methods typically available in the backcountry, sometimes your soups, sauces, and even your entrees end up too watery. Try any of the following ingredients to thicken your food: flour, potato flakes, an egg and milk powder mix, or even instant cereals. We like to mix them into a paste with water and then add them. It prevents, or at least limits, the chance of lumps. This works for tomato powder as well.

Speeding Up Cooking Time

- Choose a sheltered spot for the stove and use a windshield, especially if it's windy. Heating the outdoors with a one-burner stove is a big project, and you'll get hungry while you try. Many stoves are packaged with a windshield, or you can purchase them separately. Using the convection dome (or "Pot Parka") from Backpacker's Pantry also traps heat, and some pot sets are marketed with an optional heat exchanger. These can save a lot of time and fuel, especially on cold, high-altitude trips.

- Cooking with a lid cuts down on cooking time. Don't lift the lid or stir too often. This reduces the temperature, and therefore the cooking time is longer.

- Presoaking dehydrated vegetables and beans throughout the day can save time. A water bottle works well for this. If you overhydrate hash browns, they turn to mush. To test for hydration, break a portion in half and look for dryness in the middle. If it's dry it's not hydrated. *Do not presoak pasta!*

Preventing Burnage

- If you are a beginner, the best way to prevent burning is to make sure you don't leave the kitchen while you're cooking. A watched pot will boil, despite claims otherwise . . . even claims in this book.

- Make sure you use plenty of water. You can always add thickener later. Bring dishes to a boil, then reduce them to a simmer and stir occasionally. Add more water if you need it. Sticky is better than burnt.

- Milk and cheese like to burn, so add them last and watch them carefully.

- Margarine and oil burn less readily than butter. Margarine also spoils less readily than butter, so it's doubly good.

- When you're frying, it's okay to add a little water to help cook the ingredients and prevent burning. It cuts down on the crispy factor.

- To prevent burning when baking, make sure your stove is on a low simmer and rotate the Fry-Bake pan frequently. To adjust the heat, hold your hand about 10 inches over the flame. You should be able to keep your hand there but still feel the heat. Keep as much heat as you want on the top of the pan while baking. Oil and flour the bottom of the fry-bake pan liberally. If you start to smell a strong, wonderful aroma—or burning—it's time to check.

Preventing Accidents

- Keep everyone but the cook out of the kitchen. If it's too crowded, people kick things over and dinner ends up in the dirt. Even worse, boiling water ends up in someone's lap or boot.

- If you have to cook under a tarp or tent vestibule, at least fill and light your stove somewhere far away. Nylon melts really quickly, even when it's raining. And ventilate the cook area well. Dying from carbon monoxide poisoning puts a damper on future trips.

- Keep water handy. Twiggy fires gone wild and stoves kicked over can burn down the forest and you with it.

- Don't pour hot water in handheld containers. Burns are one of the leading causes of backcountry evacuations.

- Don't use your leg or any other part of your body as a cutting board. When using a knife, cut away from yourself.

- Fill your stove after every meal. If you have an emergency, your stove will always be ready.

Tips for Cold-Weather Cooking

- Camp early. Cooking in the cold darkness lowers the fun factor. It also makes it harder to cook effectively.

- Shelter is even more important in the cold. If there's deep snow on the ground, stamping or digging out a kitchen area (that can be filled in when you leave) not only makes a great, sheltered place to cook, but it warms you up at the same time.

- Make a lot of hot drinks. They're a great source of calories, and they make people happy.

- Bring a light pair of gloves to wear while cooking. When it's "wicked" cold, merely touching your stove can cause a nasty tissue injury. Avoid spilling fuel on flesh, which can cause rapid frostbite.

- Wipe the snow off the pots before placing them on the stove. The water dripping on the burner causes flame inconsistencies.

- Cut your cheese, meats, and margarine into chunks before leaving home. Even if they freeze solid, you can still break off some chunks . . . probably.

- Put your munchables in the inside pocket of your parka. Food might thaw by snacktime.

- When melting snow for water, always keep some starter water. Snow melts faster in water. There is more surface area.

- Go to bed with a quart of hot chocolate. It's fun to snuggle up to, and you can drink it in the night for a calorie boost.

- Sleep with snacks. (Watch out in grizzly country.) Those twelve-hour winter nights are a long time to go without eating.

Breakfasts

"No Time for Breakfast" Breakfasts

BUGG'S ALPINE START
(SERVES 1)

$^2/_3$ cup potato flakes

2–3 Tbs. dry milk

1 glob margarine

Garlic powder, chili powder, salt, and pepper to taste

$^2/_3$–$^3/_4$ cup hot water

$^1/_4$ cup cheese in small bits

HELPFUL HINTS: Heat water, milk, and margarine. Stir in potatoes and cheese until just moist. Let stand for 30 to 60 seconds. Add spices and eat.

QUESADILLAS A LA TAMAH
(SERVES 3–4)

1 dozen flour tortillas

1 lb. pepper jack cheese, shredded at home

HELPFUL HINTS: Fiddle with your stove for 10 minutes while swearing. Look for your stove-cleaning kit and then realize you left it at home. Prime your stove and then realize there is only a little fuel left in it so you will have to start all over again. Heat your frying pan (over that stove you love so much). Put a tortilla in the pan; put some cheese on the tortilla. Wait for the cheese to melt. Fold the tortilla in half, pull it out of the pan, and eat it immediately while telling your partner that the next one is his or hers.

STYLE POINTS: Add hydrated tomatoes or green pepper. Or salsa.

Thanks to Tamah V. Donaldson, Cal Adventures, Berkeley, California

BREAKFAST IN BED

1 cup quick oatmeal

4 Tbs. dry milk

Small handful raisins and nuts

½ Tbs. brown sugar

2 cups boiling water

HELPFUL HINTS: Make it in a thermos before bedding down. Snuggle up to the thermos in your sleeping bag, and in the morning you have breakfast in bed. The cereal will stay relatively warm if you make it in a water bottle that has an insulated cover. Hey, it's better than getting up!

STYLE POINTS: Convince someone to bring you a cup of hot chocolate.

LEFTOVERS

Make too much dinner and refry it in the morning. But remember, bacteria loves to grow on food, so this only works when it's really cold.

BAGELS

Bagels fried in butter and topped with cheese.

INSTANT SOUP

And the bread or biscuits you baked before going to bed. Grill the bread in your frying pan.

INSTANT BREAKFASTS

These powdered drinks are widely available at supermarkets. They don't fend off hunger and weakness for very long, but they can give you a start. Try mixing them with hot water.

CEREAL: COLD

Cold cereal can be a nutritious, high-fiber start to a backcountry day. We like to carry Grape-Nuts, Shredded Wheat, granola, and, sometimes, Raisin Bran. They can be mixed with fruit, dry milk, and water for a quick jump start in the morning.

HELPFUL HINTS: Mix the dry milk thoroughly into the cereal before adding the water. It prevents clumping. Mix two cereals together for variety. We like to eat our cold cereal hot. Just pour hot water on the top and eat away. Pick cereals that can be used in other ways, such as baking. Grape-Nuts, for instance, make a great quick crust if you don't have graham crackers.

BARB'S GRANOLA: MAKE AT HOME

5 cups oatmeal

$^1/_2$ cup raw cashews

1 cup almonds

1 cup sesame seeds

1 cup unsweetened coconut

1 cup wheat flour or soy flour

1 cup noninstant powdered milk

1 cup wheat germ

1 cup raisins

1 cup honey

1 cup vegetable oil

HELPFUL HINTS: Combine all dry ingredients. Mix honey and oil together. Blend dry with wet ingredients. Put on 2 baking trays. Bake at 325 degrees F for 10 minutes. Cool and package.

Thanks to Barb Harper, Gunnison, Colorado, and Lori Patin, Parlin, Colorado.

BACKCOUNTRY PAN-FRIED GRANOLA
(SERVES 3–4)

3 cups oatmeal

3–4 Tbs. margarine

$^1/_2$ cup brown sugar

$^1/_2$–1 cup nuts, chopped into bits

$^1/_2$–1 cup raisins

HELPFUL HINTS: Melt margarine in frying pan. Add sugar and stir aggressively until it melts. Be careful: It likes to burn. (Try tipping the pan on edge and removing it from flame if sugar starts to burn.) Add all remaining ingredients and fry until brown.

STYLE POINTS: Add a couple of tablespoons of peanut butter and serve as a trail snack late in the trip after everyone has gobbled the gorp.

CEREAL: HOT

Although hot cereals have a bad name in many circles, they really can be a warm, tasty way to start the morning, and they are quick. Many people are turned off by their appearance and name. Stop calling them gruel, mush, and bloatmeal and you'll have a lot easier time choking them down. You might even hear: "Please sir, I'd like some more."

PORRIDGE WITH A TWIST
(SERVES 2)

1 cup oats (noninstant)

2 cups water

¼ cup dry milk

Dash salt (optional)

¼ cup raisins

¼ cup dried chopped apples (or any fruit)

¼ cup chopped nuts

½ tsp. cinnamon

Sugar to taste

1 glob margarine

HELPFUL HINTS: Bring oatmeal, dry milk, fruit, salt, and water to a boil. Simmer, stirring frequently, until porridge is the desired consistency. Top with margarine, sugar, cinnamon, and nuts. Takes about 10 minutes once water boils.

STYLE POINTS: We like to substitute ¼ cup Grape-Nuts or Shredded Wheat for ¼ cup of the oatmeal. It gives it a different texture.

Popular Variations on the Theme

CREAM OF WHEAT
Substitute 2 cups cream of wheat for oatmeal. Follow directions for Porridge with a Twist.

BREAKFAST COUSCOUS / BULGUR / RICE / GRITS
Substitute any of the preceding grains for oatmeal and follow the directions for Porridge with a Twist. Mixing different types together is always a hit. These take a little longer to cook.

CORNMEAL PUDDING
Substitute 1 cup of cornmeal and 4 cups of water for the 1 cup of oatmeal and 2 cups of water in Porridge with a Twist. Proceed with the remaining directions.

INSTANT HOT CEREAL
Oatmeal, cream of wheat or rice, Malt-O-Meal/et cetera. Instant cereals usually require equal amounts of hot water and cereal. Boil water, add cereal, simmer 1 minute, and set aside. Add desired amounts of sugar, fruit, nuts, and spices.

Eggs for Breakfast

Fresh eggs will keep for a couple of weeks without refrigeration if they are not cracked. Backpacking without breaking them is almost impossible (unless you buy one of those plastic egg cases), but we've had some luck carrying them on paddling trips if they're carefully packed and used early. Most of the outdoor food companies package either powdered or freeze-dried egg breakfasts. We have tried most of these and find that they actually work. Because the portions are small, we prefer to combine them with things (potatoes, rice) rather than eat them separately. Egg powder can also be purchased in bulk so you can add your own spices and choose your own portions. We carry egg powder but use it mostly for baking. Don't try to use freeze-dried eggs in baking. They don't work.

SCRAMBLED EGGS

$^1/_2$ cup egg powder

$^1/_4$ cup dry milk

1 cup water

Margarine

Spices

HELPFUL HINTS: Mix all ingredients thoroughly. Scramble in margarine. Add spices to taste.

MOM'S IMPOSSIBLE QUICHE

$^1/_2$ cup egg powder

$^1/_4$ cup dry milk

$^1/_2$ cup water

1–2 cups filling (hydrated veggies or meat)

1 cup sliced cheese

$^3/_4$ cup Essential Batter Mix (see Backcountry Baking) or commercial mix

Spices to taste

HELPFUL HINTS: Mix together egg powder, dry milk, Essential Batter Mix, and water. Spread filling in the bottom of fry-bake pan, cover with sliced cheese, and add mixture. Stove-top bake for 20 to 30 minutes.

STYLE POINTS: Place the filling and the mixture on top of a piecrust (see Backcountry Baking).

Thanks fo Elaine Dube, Kennebunk, Maine

Potatoes for Breakfast

ESSENTIAL HASH BROWNS
(SERVES 2–3)

2 cups dried hash browns

3 Tbs. margarine

1 cup sliced cheese

Chili powder, garlic powder, and pepper to taste

1 ⅓ cups water

HELPFUL HINTS: Combine water, potatoes, and margarine in a nonstick skillet. Cook uncovered until all the water has been absorbed and bottom is brown. Flip with a spatula. Add spices and cheese. Cover until cheese has melted and the bottom is brown. Don't stir these. They will turn to mush and the bottom won't brown.

Popular Variations on the Theme

SCRAMBLED POTATOES AND EGGS
(SERVES 2–3)

2 cups dried hash browns

½ cup egg powder

¼ cup dry milk

2 ⅓ cups water

3–4 Tbs. margarine

Garlic, chili powder, black pepper to taste

1 cup sliced cheese

HELPFUL HINTS: Follow Essential Hash Browns recipe. While browns are hydrating in frying pan, mix egg powder and dry milk with 1 cup water. As hydrated browns begin to fry, mix in eggs, add spices, and scramble. More margarine may be needed. Pull off heat, top with cheese, and cover. When cheese is melted, serve.

STYLE POINTS: Carry one of the many scrambled egg or omelet mixes available through outdoor food companies. Substitute mix for egg mixture and spices. This works well with rice, too.

Truly Gourmet

BROCK'S BEANS AND BROWNS
(SERVES 4)

2 cups dried hash browns and 4 cups hot water

1 cup instant refried beans and 1 cup hot water

1 1/2 cups sliced cheese

1/4 cup egg powder, 1/2 cup water, 2 Tbs. dry milk, 1/4 cup flour, mixed

2 Tbs. margarine

Garlic powder, chili powder, black pepper, and cayenne to taste

HELPFUL HINTS: Hydrate browns and beans separately. Mix egg/milk/water/flour slurry into hydrated potatoes and pour them into the fry-bake pan atop the melted margarine. Position sliced cheese over the potatoes and top with beans/spice mixture. Stove-top bake 20 minutes or until done. Eggs must cook and cheese must melt. If you're in a rush, this recipe works well if you merely roll the crisped browns, cheese, and beans into a tortilla.

STYLE POINTS: Crisp the browns before baking. Serve with hot sauce, tortillas, sprouts, and sour cream.

Thanks to Mark Stivers, Lander, Wyoming, and Kate Bartlett, Elaine Doll, Brett LeCompte, and Steve Mital of the Deer Hill School, Mancos, Colorado.

MARBLE MOUNTAIN MORNING CAKES
(MAKES 4–6 CAKES)

1 lb. dehydrated hash browns

1/4 lb. cheese

1/8 cup whole-wheat flour

1/8 cup cornmeal

Raspberry jelly or preserves

HELPFUL HINTS: Cover potatoes with about 6 to 8 cups of boiling water. Set aside to hydrate (about 10 minutes). Be careful not to oversoak the potatoes or else they get soggy. Drain potatoes, saving a little water in the bottom. Add flour and cornmeal to mixture until you have a stiff batter. Form and flatten a cake in an oiled frying pan. Cook at medium-high heat, flipping when one side browns. After you flip, put a slice of cheese on the cake and add the lid onto the pan to melt the cheese. Serve topped with raspberry jelly syrup.

Thanks to Michael Hock, Santa Fe, New Mexico.

ESSENTIAL PANCAKES

(SERVES 2–4)

2 cups Essential Batter Mix (see Backcountry Baking)

¼ cup egg powder (optional)

1 Tbs. sugar (optional)

About 2 ¼ cups water

HELPFUL HINTS: Remember to adjust batter for the altitude (see Backcountry Baking). Slowly mix water into the dry ingredients until batter pours easily off spoon. If it's too thin, add more flour. Pour batter into bottom of a heated, oiled frying pan. Cook over medium heat until bubbles form on the top of the cake. Flip and cook until cake is golden brown and sounds hollow when tapped.

STYLE POINTS: Substitute buttermilk powder for milk powder in the Essential Batter Mix. Or add chopped nuts to the batter.

Popular Variations on the Theme

GRANOLA PANCAKES

1 ½ cups Essential Batter Mix (see Backcountry Baking)

½ cup granola

¼ cup egg powder (optional)

About 2 cups water

HELPFUL HINTS: Follow directions for Essential Pancakes.

APPLE PANCAKES

2 cups Essential Batter Mix (see Backcountry Baking)

1 pkg. hot apple cider mix

1 pkg. instant applesauce

¼ cup egg powder (optional)

About 2 ¼ cups water

HELPFUL HINTS: Follow the directions for Essential Pancakes.

STYLE POINTS: Add ½ cup of hydrated apple pieces to batter.

WILD AND HOTCAKES

2 cups Essential Batter Mix (see Backcountry Baking)

1 cup wild berries

2 Tbs. sugar

2–4 Tbs. egg powder (optional)

About 2 cups water

HELPFUL HINTS: Follow the directions for Essential Pancakes.

STYLE POINTS: Serve with Pick Your Own Syrup (from later in this chapter).

CORN GRIDDLE CAKES

1 ½ cups cornmeal

½ cup whole-wheat flour

2 tsps. baking powder

2 Tbs. oil

1 Tbs. sugar

⅓ cup dry milk

About 2 cups water

HELPFUL HINTS: Slowly mix the water and oil into the dry ingredients. Cook as described in Essential Pancakes.

STYLE POINTS: Hydrate 1 cup of dried corn and add it to the batter before cooking.

BLOATMEAL PANCAKES

1 cup oatmeal

⅓ cup dry milk

2 Tbs. oil

½ cup flour

2 tsps. baking powder

1 Tbs. sugar (optional)

¼ cup egg powder (optional)

About 2 cups water

HELPFUL HINTS: Combine oatmeal, oil, and water in pan and let it stand for 5 to 10 minutes to soften oats. Stir in the dry ingredients. Flip-bake as described under Essential Pancakes.

STYLE POINTS are rewarded to anyone who utilizes oatmeal in anything but a gruel.

CHOCOLATE LOVER'S PANCAKES

2 cups Essential Batter Mix (see Backcountry Baking)

1/4 cup egg powder (optional)

1/4 cup cocoa or 1/2 cup hot chocolate mix

Chocolate or carob chips

About 2 1/4 cups water

HELPFUL HINTS: Follow the directions for Essential Pancakes.

HEALTH CAKES

(SERVES 3–4)

2/3 cup whole-wheat flour

1/3 cup white flour

1/4 cup oatmeal or cornmeal

2 Tbs. wheat germ or bran

1 Tbs. sugar

2 tsps. baking powder

2 Tbs. egg powder

4 Tbs. buttermilk powder

1 Tbs. oil

About 1 1/2 cups water

HELPFUL HINTS: Mix all dry ingredients. Slowly add oil and water. Cook as described in Essential Pancakes.

Pancake Toppings

QUICK TOPPINGS

#1: Brown sugar and margarine.

#2: Jelly.

#3: Instant applesauce.

#4: Peanut butter.

CINNAMON BUTTER

1/2 cup sugar

1/2 tsp. cinnamon

1/4 cup margarine

HONEY BUTTER

¼ *cup margarine*

⅛ *cup honey*

BASIC SYRUP

½ *cup sugar*

¼ *cup water*

¼ *cup margarine*

HELPFUL HINTS: Simmer in small pan until sugar is dissolved and keep warm. Remember: Sugar likes to burn.

STYLE POINTS: Add a tsp. of vanilla or a dash of cinnamon.

Popular Variations on the Theme

PICK YOUR OWN SYRUP

2 *cups wild berries*

½ *cup sugar*

Water

HELPFUL HINTS: Pick the berry of your choice or any edible berry you can find. Simmer berries with sugar, smashing as you stir. Add water to desired consistency. Some berries require more sugar than others. For example, currants aren't very sweet, while grouse whortleberries are very sweet. Add a little flour as thickener if you need it.

STYLE POINTS: Be able to distinguish good berries from bad berries.

HONEY SYRUP

1 *cup honey*

1 *tsp. vanilla*

2 *Tbs. water*

2 *Tbs. margarine*

½ *cup coconut*

HELPFUL HINTS: Heat all ingredients to desired consistency.

APPLE SYRUP

¹/₂ cup sugar

¹/₂ cup water

1 pkg. hot apple cider mix

HELPFUL HINTS: Heat ingredients to desired consistency.

JELLY SYRUP

¹/₂ cup jelly

3 Tbs. margarine

HELPFUL HINTS: Heat ingredients to desired consistency.

Truly Something

THE EYE-OPENER SYRUP

2 cups strong coffee

¹/₂ cup sugar

HELPFUL HINTS: Boil coffee continuously. Add sugar a spoonful at a time and stir. Boil until almost a syrup. It will thicken as it cools down. Pour over your pancakes for the best darn syrup you'll ever have outside of New England.

Thanks to David Tomco, Glastonbury, Connecticut.

Breakfast Breads

Don't put more than 2 to 2 ¹/₂ cups of batter into a 9- to 10-inch fry-bake pan because it will rise up and stick to lid. Adjust recipes for altitude (see Backcountry Baking).

SIN-A-MON BISCUITS

2 cups Essential Batter Mix or any commercially available mix

¹/₂ cup dry milk

¹/₂ cup oats (or leftover oatmeal)

¹/₂ cup brown sugar

2 tsps. cinnamon

1 handful raisins

³/₄ cup water

HELPFUL HINTS: Combine dry ingredients and mix with wet. Fold gently until mixed. Bake in an oiled, heated, covered skillet until brown on one side. Flip and bake until brown.

Thanks to J. Scott McGee, Richmond, Oregon.

PSEUDOSCONES

1 ½ cups Essential Batter Mix (see Backcountry Baking)

½ cup flour

½ cup raisins

¼ cup brown sugar

2 Tbs. egg powder (optional)

1 tsp. ground ginger

½ tsp. cinnamon

¼ tsp. nutmeg

About ¾ cup water

HELPFUL HINTS: Mix all ingredients into a stiff dough. Press into the bottom of a greased frying pan. Cut dough with a spatula into 6 to 12 triangles. Stove-top bake.

STYLE POINTS: Serve with cinnamon sugar or orange fruit crystals sprinkled on the top.

FRUITY FRITTERS

1 ½ cups Essential Batter Mix (see Backcountry Baking)

2 Tbs. egg powder (optional)

¾ cup water

1 Tbs. sugar

1 cup dried chopped apples (or whatever)

½ tsp. cinnamon or nutmeg

HELPFUL HINTS: Hydrate apples. Combine all ingredients. Drop by spoonfuls into a hot frying pan. Fry in oil until crispy brown.

ESSENTIAL COFFEE CAKE

(SERVES 4)

2 cups Essential Batter Mix (see Backcountry Baking)

4–8 Tbs. sugar

2 Tbs. egg powder

½ tsp. salt

2 Tbs. oil or melted margarine

1 cup water

HELPFUL HINTS: Mix all dry ingredients in a pan. Add the wet ingredients slowly until most of the lumps are gone. Scrape the batter into an oiled fry-bake pan. Cover the batter with one of the toppings below (or your own) and stove-top bake for 20 to 30 minutes.

STYLE POINTS: Add 1 package of sour cream mix to the dry ingredients and 1 teaspoon of vanilla to the wet. Top with the Essential Coffee Cake Topping but use pecans as the nut.

TOPPING

½ cup brown sugar

1–2 tsp. cinnamon

2 Tbs. melted margarine

½ cup nuts (walnuts or almonds are good)

2 Tbs. flour or oatmeal (we prefer oatmeal)

HELPFUL HINTS: Mix all ingredients in a small pan or bowl and spread as best you can on top of the cake prior to baking it.

WILD MORNING COFFEE CAKE

(SERVES 4)

Follow Essential Coffee Cake recipe for batter.

STYLE POINTS: Substitute dry buttermilk for dry milk in Essential Batter Mix.

TOPPING

2 cups berries (anything nonpoisonous will do)

1 cup dry milk

¼–⅓ sugar (currants need a lot of sugar)

HELPFUL HINTS: Mix all ingredients together. Spoon on top of cake and stove-top bake.

Truly Gourmet
MORNING STREUSEL

THE BATTER

1 1/2 cups flour

2 tsps. baking powder

1/4 tsp. salt

1/2 cup sugar

4 Tbs. margarine

2 Tbs. egg powder

2 Tbs. dry buttermilk or milk

3/4 cup water

HELPFUL HINTS: Combine all dry ingredients and then mix in the wet ones slowly. Pour half of mixture into an oiled fry-bake pan. Sprinkle with half of filling. Add other half of batter and filling. Stove-top bake for 20 to 30 minutes or until done.

THE FILLING

2 Tbs. flour

2 tsps. cinnamon

1/2 cup brown sugar

2 Tbs. melted margarine

1/2 cup chopped nuts

HELPFUL HINTS: Mix together in a bowl and set aside until needed.

YEAST CINNAMON SPIRAL

Make Essential Yeast Bread (see Backcountry Baking)

FILLING

2 Tbs. flour

2 tsp. cinnamon

1/2 cup brown sugar

2 Tbs. melted margarine

1/2 cup chopped nuts

HELPFUL HINTS: Using your water bottle, roll dough into a thin rectangle on top of a plastic bag (more hygienic) or your foam-lite pad (less hygienic). Cover the rectangle with the filling, leaving about an inch around the edges. Roll dough into a tight tube and seal-pinch edges closed. If edges won't seal, dab a little water on them. Coil the dough into a spiral starting in the center of your fry-bake pan and working outward. If dough doesn't fill pan completely, press it firmly into the bottom until it does. Stove-top bake until done, about 30 minutes.

If you're in a rush you can flip-bake (see Backcountry Baking), but the end product is denser.

STYLE POINTS: Cut rolled tube into 1- to 2-inch rounds and stove-top bake circles flat for cinnamon rolls (see Backcountry Baking).

Munchables

Munchables—some people refer to them as lunchables—should total about 20 percent of your total food weight. Supermarkets, health food stores, and outdoor food companies provide a wide enough variety of these items to please almost anyone. Below we've listed some of our favorites in terms of taste and durability.

BREADS AND CRACKERS
Bagels, tortillas, pita bread, pilot biscuits, melba toast, bagel chips, rye crisps, or any hardy cracker.

TRAIL MIXES
Trail mixes are widely available in a variety of mixtures. Over the years we've phased them out of our diet in favor of carrying items individually and then mixing them in small amounts. Why? We spent too many dimly lit evenings picking things out of the mixes to use in baking, like the chocolate chips, and we grew tired of traveling companions "mining" the M&Ms out of the gorp. Buy trail mixes if you're in a rush, or build your own if you're picky about the contents.

MEAT, PEANUT BUTTER, AND CHEESE
These items are usually represented in the 13 percent of your total weight entitled *high-calorie*. They make great munchables, especially on cool-weather trips. The harder cheeses (Cheddar, Swiss, Colby, Edam, Gouda) last longer without spoiling. If you leave the cheese vacuum-packed until you're ready to eat, it won't mold. Many summer sausages and pepperoni need no refrigeration until the casing is broken. Buy them in small packages and plan to share them at one lunch or dinner. Peanut butter is high calorie but has no cholesterol. It's not as versatile as meat or cheese, but it's good for variety. Peanut butter is also good in soups, sauces, and breads.

DRIED FRUITS AND NUTS
Carry them separately or toss them into trail mixes. They are high calorie for their weight.

FRESH FRUITS AND VEGETABLES
Hardy fruits and vegetables make great snacks, but they're not light. We often carry apples and carrots.

CANDY AND GRANOLA BARS
Remember, chocolate melts in the heat. Hard candies are occasionally nice to have in your pocket, especially for energy snacks on the go.

COOKIES
We usually carry fruit bars. They're high calorie but low fat, and if you crush them it doesn't matter . . . they just clump together. Whatever you like, try to pick cookies that won't immediately turn to dust if you stuff your sleeping bag onto them. If you discover dust, use it to make a no-bake pie, or dump the crumbs into a pudding.

JERKY
Although it's hard to find, salmon jerky is our favorite. Jerky can also be hydrated and added to meals.

ENERGY BARS AND DRINKS
We carry them. They're low fat and a nice boost for that last couple of miles to camp.

Munchables to Make in the Backcountry
It doesn't seem to matter how many munchables you bring with you, they will be gone before the end of your trip. Don't berate your companions for eating more than their share of the trail mix. Impress them with your ability to take the bits and pieces of the remaining stores and turn them into tasty treats.

SCOOBY-SNACKS
Follow the Essential Pan Biscuits recipe (see Backcountry Baking). Sweeten the biscuits with sugar and raisins or add some nuts. Leftover crumbs of cookies or graham crackers combine nicely. Top them with cheese, peanut butter, or margarine, or eat them alone.

Thanks to Dan Robison, Block Island, Rhode Island.

INSTANT SOUPS AND INSTANT POTATOES
A quick lunch if you can spare the time to boil water. Ramen noodles only take 3 minutes once the water has boiled. This is an especially nice break on a cold, windy day.

Pan-Fried Granola (see Breakfasts), **Pan Biscuits, Sweet Breads, and Cakes** (see Backcountry Baking) can become lunch.

Munchables to Make at Home

After cooking any of the bars described below, cool them thoroughly in the refrigerator, then cut them and freeze them until use. If you don't cool and freeze them, they tend to break apart and get eaten at home!

SOLO BARS

6 eggs

1 lb. brown sugar

1 lb. white sugar

$\frac{1}{2}$ tsp. vanilla extract

4 tsps. baking soda

$\frac{1}{2}$ lb. butter

1 $\frac{1}{2}$ lbs. crunchy peanut butter

9 cups oatmeal

1 lb. chocolate chips

$\frac{1}{2}$ lb. raisins

Sunflower seeds

1 cup shredded coconut (keeps the bars moist)

HELPFUL HINTS: Mix in order given. Bake on 2 jelly-roll sheets at 350 degrees F until done. Sides will pull away and become golden brown. Don't overcook or they become hard and crispy instead of thick and chewy.

Thanks to Ruthe Hubbell, Conway, New Hampshire

FRUIT BARS

1 cup chopped walnuts

$\frac{1}{2}$ cup raisins

$\frac{1}{2}$ cup dried apricots

$\frac{1}{3}$ cup orange juice

1 $\frac{1}{2}$ cups flour

$\frac{1}{2}$ tsp. baking powder

$\frac{1}{2}$ tsp. salt

$\frac{1}{2}$ tsp. cinnamon

$\frac{1}{2}$ cup butter

$\frac{1}{2}$ cup brown sugar

2 eggs

1 cup diced candied fruit

GLAZE

1 cup powdered sugar

1 Tbs. hot water

1 1/2 tsps. melted butter

1/4 cup finely diced candied fruit

HELPFUL HINTS: Cut apricots into small pieces and combine with raisins and orange juice. Sift together flour, baking powder, salt, and cinnamon and set aside. Cream together butter, sugar, and brown sugar. Beat in 2 eggs. Stir in fruit mixture and flour mixture. Stir in walnuts and candied fruit. Spread in a 9- by 13-inch pan and bake at 375 degrees F until done. Cool and spread with Glaze.

DEEP IN THE CONGO BARS

2 3/4 cups flour

2 1/2 tsps. baking powder

1/2 tsp. salt

2/3 cup shortening or butter

1 lb. dark brown sugar

3 eggs

1 cup chopped walnuts or pecans

1/2 lb. chocolate chips

HELPFUL HINTS: Mix baking powder, flour, and salt. Melt shortening and add brown sugar. Allow it to cool slightly and add eggs. Beat well. Add dry ingredients. Stir in chips and nuts. Bake at 350 degrees F for 25 to 30 minutes.

SEVEN SUMMITS BAR

1/2 stick butter

1 cup graham cracker crumbs

1 cup shredded coconut

2 cups mixed chocolate and butterscotch chips

1 can sweetened condensed milk

3/4 cup oatmeal

1 cup chopped walnuts

HELPFUL HINTS: Layer in a 9- by 13-inch pan in the order listed and bake at 350 degrees F for 20 minutes. Cool thoroughly, cut into bars, and freeze until ready to use.

SPLIT-LEVEL RUINS

(RUINS YOUR APPETITE)

1 cup chocolate chips

3 oz. cream cheese

$^1\!/_3$ cup evaporated milk

$^1\!/_2$ cup chopped walnuts

2 Tbs. sesame seeds

$^1\!/_2$ tsp. almond extract

1$^1\!/_2$ cups flour

$^1\!/_2$ tsp. baking powder

$^1\!/_4$ tsp. salt

$^3\!/_4$ cup sugar

$^1\!/_2$ cup soft margarine

1 egg

$^1\!/_2$ cup oatmeal

HELPFUL HINTS: Melt together chocolate, cream cheese, and milk over low heat. Stir constantly. Remove from heat and stir in walnuts, seeds, and almond extract. Combine remaining ingredients and press them into the bottom of an oiled baking pan (8 by 11 inches). Pour chocolate mixture on the top and spread evenly. Sprinkle with oatmeal. Bake at 375 degrees F until done, about 20 minutes. Cool.

QUEST BREAD

4 cups whole-wheat flour

$^1\!/_3$ cup wheat germ

$^3\!/_4$ cup brown sugar

$^1\!/_3$ cup oil

$^1\!/_4$ cup molasses

4 Tbs. dry milk

1$^1\!/_2$ tsps. salt

1$^1\!/_2$ tsps. baking powder

$^1\!/_4$ cup sunflower seeds

1 cup water

HELPFUL HINTS: Combine all ingredients and mix thoroughly. Bake in an oiled 8- by 8-inch pan at 300 degrees F for approximately 1 hour. Cool, cut into squares, and put in a plastic bag. Make sure bread is cool and dry when you package it. This bread will last for weeks without growing mold.

NUTTY TREATS

Nuts are high in calories and a great source of protein. Unfortunately, they are also a great source of fat. But it's mostly monounsaturated fat (except in coconut; that's why it's so moist and tasty), and they have no cholesterol. Mix nuts into snacks for a nutritional boost.

GOOP BALLS
(OR JUST GOOP)

About 1 cup peanut butter

$^{1}/_{2}$ cup granola

$^{1}/_{2}$ cup dry milk

$^{1}/_{4}$ cup brown sugar

$^{1}/_{4}$ cup raisins

$^{1}/_{2}$ cup chopped nuts

HELPFUL HINTS: Mix granola, milk, sugar, raisins, and nuts in a bowl or pan. Add enough peanut butter to make the mixture stiff but not crumbly. Roll into golf balls and store chilled. You can also mix this in a plastic bag and eat it by the spoonful for lunch.

STYLE POINTS: Roll balls in coconut before serving. Add chocolate chips instead of nuts.

SPICED NUTS

2 cups unsalted dry-roasted nuts

1–2 Tbs. hot sesame oil

1–2 Tbs. garlic tamari (or soy sauce and $^{1}/_{8}$ tsp. garlic powder)

$^{1}/_{2}$ tsp. cayenne

HELPFUL HINTS: Mix all ingredients together in a bowl. Spread them on a baking sheet and bake at 350 degrees F for 30 minutes. Stir them 2 or 3 times while baking. Allow nuts to cool and then package them in a plastic container.

NUBBLES
(NUTS AND NIBBLES)

4–5 cups dry cereal (Crispex, Fruit Wheats, Rice/Wheat/Corn Chex, etc.)

1 cup unsalted pretzels, broken into bits

2 cups unsalted dry-roasted nuts

$^{1}/_{3}$ cup margarine

$1^{1}/_{2}$ Tbs. Worcestershire sauce

1 tsp. onion powder

1/2–1 tsp. garlic powder

1 tsp. celery flakes

HELPFUL HINTS: Heat margarine, Worcestershire, and spices. Add to cereal-pretzel mixture and mix. Add nuts and stir. Bake at 300 degrees F on a baking sheet for 10 minutes.

STYLE POINTS: Okay, add chocolate bits after the mixture cools.

MA'S SUGARY PEANUTS

4 cups raw, shelled peanuts

2 cups sugar

1 cup water

HELPFUL HINTS: Mix sugar and water in a large frying pan. Add peanuts and bring to a boil. Simmer for 15 to 20 minutes until the liquid crystallizes on the nuts. Spread on a baking sheet and bake at 325 degrees F for 15 minutes.

STYLE POINTS: Add a teaspoon of flavoring: vanilla, chocolate, or the like.

Thanks to Eris Mozingo Tilton, Putney, Georgia.

HOMEMADE JERKY

2 lbs. meat (very lean beef, elk, deer, salmon, etc.)

1/2 cup soy sauce or tamari

1/2 cup Worcestershire sauce

1/2 tsp. garlic powder or crushed garlic

1 tsp. meat tenderizer

Optional: salt, onion salt, pepper, oregano, basil, thyme, marjoram, or whatever

HELPFUL HINTS: Partially freeze the meat so it's easier to slice into strips no more than 1/2 inch thick—even thinner is better. Trim away any visible fat. The higher the quality of the meat, the higher the quality of the jerky. Mix the wet ingredients with garlic and meat tenderizer to make the marinade. Gently rub the meat with the desired spices, but use at least a little salt and pepper. Soak the meat in the marinade, in the refrigerator, for at least 24 hours. Drain and then dry the meat with a paper towel. Place the strips evenly on an oven rack, not touching each other, and turn the oven on to about 150 degrees F. The meat will drip, so you might be happier later if you spread a layer of foil on the bottom of the oven. Leave the door of the oven slightly open for better circulation. You'll have black, nasty-looking, excellent-tasting jerky in about 7 or 8 hours—maybe less if you sliced the meat really thin.

Sauces

G rains, pasta, and potatoes are just, well, carbohydrates without sauce. Sauce is like a pinch of salt on an egg, salsa on tortilla chips, frosting on a cake—or, for the analogically challenged, sauce is necessary. Who, for instance, can stomach couscous or bulgur without a sauce? You know that carbohydrates power you around the backcountry, but it's the sauces that make them tasty meals, turn food into an event. All it takes is a little forethought, a few extra ounces in your backpack, and about five more minutes.

Although mixing and matching is allowed, even encouraged—hey, who knows what will appeal to your taste buds—white (cream) sauces are generally preferred on pastas, grains, and rehydrated vegetables; red (tomato) sauces and green (pesto) sauces on pasta; and brown sauces (called "gravy" by some) on potatoes and vegetables. Specialty sauces, such as those flavored with curry or peanut butter (see below), go extremely well on rice, couscous, and bulgur.

Just Add Water . . . Maybe

No time (or heart) for from-scratch sauce making? Try an off-the-shelf package of premixed, powdered sauce. You can get a great brown gravy from Knorr or Schilling by adding a cup of water to the powder, bringing the slurry to a boil, and simmering for a couple of minutes.

For a premixed white sauce, you'll need to be sure you've packed some milk—and we strongly prefer Milkman, which reconstitutes easily without clumping. To get Alfredo, an especially rich cream sauce, from a package, you'll need to pack a little butter or margarine in addition to the powdered milk. The pesto sauces require a splash of oil. The basic rule of packing before a trip is simple: Read the back of the package first.

From-Scratch Sauces

With a couple of pioneering efforts on the sauce-cooking frontier, you can soon be amazing your friends, and yourself, by preparing sauces from scratch. All you need is a few extra ingredients in the food bag and a well-stocked spice kit. A huge hunk of the fun is varying the nonessential ingredients to create personal sauces.

BASIC CREAM SAUCE

(MAKES ABOUT 1 CUP)

	Thin	Medium	Thick
Milk	1 cup	1 cup	1 cup
(4 Tbs. dry & 1 cup water)			
Flour	1 Tbs.	2 Tbs.	3 Tbs.
Margarine	1 Tbs.	2 Tbs.	3 Tbs.

HELPFUL HINTS: As you can see, you can vary the measurements quite a bit and still get cream sauce, so don't worry about it too much if you don't have a measuring device. Melt margarine in bottom of pan over low heat; add flour, stirring constantly to prevent burning, until mixture is as smooth as possible. Add reconstituted milk, slowly stirring constantly to prevent burning. Keep stirring over low heat until it is thick enough. This usually takes about 5 minutes. Take it off the heat and add salt and pepper to taste.

Popular Variations on the Theme

CHEESE SAUCE

1 cup Basic Cream Sauce
½–1 cup of your favorite cheese

HELPFUL HINTS: Make the Basic Cream Sauce first; cut the cheese into small bits and add it at the end with the pot off the burner. Remember: Cheese loves to burn.

MUSTARD CHEESE SAUCE

1 cup Basic Cream Sauce
½ cup cheese
¼ tsp. garlic powder
¼ tsp. mustard powder (or 1 Tbs. mustard)
Dash cayenne or Tabasco

ALFREDO

1 cup Basic Cream Sauce
½ cup Parmesan cheese
½ tsp. basil or dill
¼ tsp. garlic
Salt and pepper to taste

BROWN GRAVY

1 cup Basic Cream Sauce

1 tsp. onion flakes

¼ tsp. garlic powder

1–2 Tbs. soy sauce or tamari

HELPFUL HINTS: Add a beef or chicken bouillon cube instead of the soy sauce for a "meat" option. Don't do both or it will be too salty. These sauces are great on pan biscuits for breakfast.

TOMATO CREAM SAUCE

1 cup Basic Cream Sauce

2 Tbs. tomato base

½ tsp. garlic powder

1 tsp. basil

HELPFUL HINTS: Use 2 cups of instant tomato soup instead of base and spices. Serve on pasta.

ASIAN TOMATO SAUCE

1 cup Basic Cream Sauce

2 Tbs. tomato base

¼ teaspoon ground ginger

1 Tbs. onion flakes

Soy sauce or tamari to your liking

HELPFUL HINTS: Serve on bulgur or rice.

Peanut Butter Sauces

PEANUT BUTTER GRAVY
(MAKES ABOUT 1½ CUPS)

½ cup peanut butter (crunchy is better)

¼ tsp. garlic powder

2 Tbs. vinegar (optional)

3 Tbs. dry milk (optional)

1 cup hot water

1½ Tbs. soy sauce

Cayenne

HELPFUL HINTS: Heat water, remove from burner, and add other ingredients. Reheat carefully if need arises. Peanut butter loves to scorch your pan. Excellent on spaghetti noodles.

HOT SESAME-PEANUT SAUCE

½ cup peanut butter (crunchy is better)

1 cup hot water

2 Tbs. vinegar (optional)

3 tsps. hot sesame oil

1½ tsps. soy sauce or tamari

1 tsp. onion flakes

½ tsp. crushed hot red pepper

HELPFUL HINTS: Heat water, remove from burner, and add other ingredients. Excellent served hot or cold over noodles.

CURRY SAUCE

1 Tbs. oil

1 Tbs. flour

2 tsp. onion flakes

1 cup water

¼ cup dried chopped apples

¼ cup raisins

1 tsp. brown sugar

1½–2 tsps. curry powder

½ tsp. salt

HELPFUL HINTS: Heat oil and flour, stirring constantly, over low heat until the mixture is smooth. Add spices, water, and fruit. Bring to a boil and simmer until apples are tender. Serve over lentils, rice, bulgur, or couscous.

ITALIAN TOMATO SAUCE

1/2 cup tomato powder

1 Tbs. onion flakes

1/2 Tbs. parsley

1/2 tsp. basil or oregano

1/2 Tbs. oil

1/4 tsp. garlic powder

1 1/2–2 cups water (more for thinner sauce)

Optional: dried tomatoes, mushrooms, peppers, etc.

HELPFUL HINTS: Bring water and any dehydrated vegetables you are using to a boil. Add the rest of the ingredients and simmer, stirring frequently, over low heat until you are satisfied with the flavoring and consistency. Great sauce for pasta, lasagna, and pizza.

MEXICAN SAUCE

2–3 Tbs. tomato powder

1 cup hot water (more for thinner sauce)

1 Tbs. onion flakes

1/2–1 tsp. chili powder

1/2 tsp. cumin

1/2 tsp. basil or oregano

1/4 tsp. garlic powder

1 Tbs. oil

1 Tbs. cornmeal or flour

Black pepper

2 Tbs. red and green peppers (optional)

Dried tomato (optional)

HELPFUL HINTS: Rehydrate vegetables in hot water. Heat oil, seasonings, and cornmeal in bottom of pan. Combine all ingredients and simmer, stirring frequently, for 5 to 10 minutes. Great on beans, rice, bulgur, or pizza.

Soups

Soups are a great pick-me-up before meals and a wonderful lunch on a cold day with breads or snacks. You can make soups quickly with the ingredients you carry in your pack, or there are lots of quick soups available at your local store or outdoor shop. We tend to stock up on instant soups at the grocery store. They are quick, inexpensive (though salty), and make great flavorings when added to grains and potatoes. Soups are also a great way to get rid of leftovers or to use up bits and pieces of food at the end of a trip.

ESSENTIAL BROTH SOUP

6 cups water

2–3 bouillon cubes or 2–3 pkgs. instant soup

¼ cup margarine

1–2 cups filler: grains, pasta, potatoes, vegetable, cheese, etc.

Spices

HELPFUL HINTS: Boil the water and add bouillon. Be careful: This is salty. Add solid ingredients and spices. Simmer until done.

Popular Mixes

MISO SOUP: Cup of miso soup, dried tofu, noodles, onion flakes, garlic powder, and black pepper.

CHICKEN SOUP: Chicken bouillon, dried vegetables, noodles or rice, and curry powder.

TOMATO BEEF: Tomato powder and beef or vegetable bouillon, dried vegetables, noodles, black pepper, basil, and garlic powder.

LENTIL SOUP: Lentils, tomato base, vegetable bouillon, onion flakes, garlic powder, cumin, chili powder, and black pepper.

Truly Gourmet

DUMPLINGS

1 cup Essential Batter Mix (see Backcountry Baking)
About ⅓ cup water

HELPFUL HINTS: Mix dry and wet ingredients. Drop batter by spoonfuls onto the top of the bubbling soup. Simmer uncovered until the dumplings are done, about 10 minutes.

STYLE POINTS: Add herbs or cheese to your dumpling batter.

ESSENTIAL CREAMY SOUP

6 cups water
2–3 bouillon cubes or 2–3 pkgs. instant soup
¼ cup margarine
1–2 cups filler: grains, pasta, potatoes, vegetables, cheese, etc.
½–1 cup dry milk
¼ cup flour or potato flakes, buds, or pearls (thickener)
Spices

HELPFUL HINTS: Bring water to boil, then add bouillon, spices, and fillers. Simmer until fillers are tender. Mix thickener into a paste with a small bit of water. Slowly add the paste to the soup, stirring constantly, until thick. Add milk and any cheese last.

Popular Mixes

TOMATO: Tomato base, rice, black pepper, oregano, garlic powder, milk, and thickener.

CHOWDER: Vegetable bouillon, dried corn and potatoes, black pepper, basil, garlic, milk, and thickener.

CREAM OF BROCCOLI: 2 pkgs. instant cream of broccoli soup, dried potatoes, and black pepper.

CREAM OF CHICKEN: 2 pkgs. instant creamy chicken vegetable soup, rice, black pepper, and thickener.

Entrees

Grains, Grains, Grains

A native grain of Asia, rice is the staple food for over half the folks in the world. There are many different types of rice sold in the United States. In terms of shapes, long-grain rice grains are approximately four times longer than they are wide and cook up very fluffy; medium-grain rices are softer and tend to cook up more tender; and short-grain rice is the stickiest.

Brown rice is the whole unpolished rice grain with only the husk and a bit of bran removed. White rice has been husked and polished, with bran and germ removed. Brown rice takes about twice as long to cook as white rice and has a nuttier, chewier flavor. Precooked or instant rice is the most expensive, the most processed, and the least nourishing. We usually cook with instant rice only in situations where we need to save fuel. Brown and white rice are now available at the local supermarket in instant and noninstant forms.

Wild rice, amazingly enough, is not really rice but the seed of a water grass native to the northern Great Lakes. It's very nutritious and a great way to add style points to any meal, in addition to being very expensive.

Bulgur is the "rice" of the Middle East. It is really not rice either, but cracked wheat that has been parboiled (steamed and dried) and cracked into small bits. You see it more commonly at supermarkets these days, but it can be readily found in bulk at health food stores and co-ops. Bulgur has a nutty flavor. It is great mixed with rice or in any recipe that calls for rice. It cooks faster than rice. People who call bulgur vulgar have not been introduced to it correctly.

Couscous is the bulgur of North Africa. It's finely cracked wheat or millet that has been parboiled and refined. It cooks very quickly.

Other grains that are available for a change of pace include: millet (takes a lot of time and water to cook), barley (available in quick-cooking form), kasha or buckwheat groats (an eastern European grain with a nutlike flavor), and corn grits (which can be hard to get outside of the South).

These days there are many companies from which to buy prepackaged grain mixtures of different flavors right at the supermarket. Several companies market meals prepared specifically for outdoor travelers. Many of these options are tasty, but they tend to be expensive and, depending on the brand you pick, can have many additives, especially salt. Unless we are traveling where time and ease of cooking are more of an issue than money and flavor, we prefer to cook our grain dishes from scratch. We often will throw a commercial mix or two in the food bag for a change of pace or at the end of a long day. If you buy commercial mixes, make sure you get at least a serving and a half per person. Ready-made mixes tend to overestimate the number of people they will serve.

ESSENTIAL GRAIN
(YIELDS ABOUT 2½–3 CUPS; SERVES 2)

1 cup grain

2 cups water (for wild rice, millet, or barley, add 3 cups)

HELPFUL HINTS: Wait for the water to boil to add the grain. (It's not required, but it makes the grain less sticky.) Simmer with pot covered so water does not evaporate before the grain is soft. Do not stir grain unless you like it sticky and clumped together. To prevent burning, tip the pot to the side periodically as the water is absorbed to assure there is a small amount of water in the bottom. If the water is gone and the grain is still crunchy, it is acceptable to add more water, preferably hot, but it's not required. Bulgur, couscous, and kasha take about 15 to 20 minutes. White rice will cook about twice as fast as brown rice (30 minutes versus 1 hour). If you prefer brown rice or barley, we suggest buying quick-cooking style, especially if you are traveling above 10,000 feet. It can take a lot of fuel at higher elevations.

SERVING SUGGESTIONS: A quick way to make basic grains more interesting is to cook them with one or two instant soups. Cream of chicken, creamy tomato, and cream of mushroom are consistent favorites. Serve with a Curry or Mexican Sauce (see Sauces). Cook grains and then fry them with nuts, herbs, and spices and a bit of leftover pasta. Cook grains, add cream sauce, top with nuts, cheese, and bread crumbs, and bake. Mixing grains together is a treat as well, but remember that some take longer to cook than others. Dried vegetables improve the appearance and sometimes the flavor of your grain dishes.

Popular Variations on the Theme

CREAMY NUT PILAF
(SERVES 2–3)

1 cup rice or bulgur

2 cups water

1 bouillon cube

1 cup Basic Cream Sauce (see Sauces)

⅓ cup Parmesan cheese

⅓ cup sunflower seeds

Salt and pepper to taste

HELPFUL HINTS: Cook rice with bouillon cube and water. Set aside. Prepare Basic Cream Sauce, adding cheese and seeds last. Season to taste.

STYLE POINTS: Include ⅓ cup of orzo pasta and ½ cup of dried mushrooms to the original cooking.

SPANISH RICE
(SERVE 2–4)

1 cup rice

2 cups water

1 bouillon cube

1 Tbs. oil

⅓ cup dried red and green peppers

1 cup dried tomatoes

2 cups instant tomato soup

1–2 Tbs. onion flakes

½ tsp. garlic powder

½ tsp. basil

½ tsp. oregano

½ tsp. chili powder

½–1 cup grated Cheddar

Black pepper and cayenne to taste

HELPFUL HINTS: Cook rice, water, onion flakes, dried peppers, tomatoes, and instant soup. Place oil in frying pan. Add rice mixture and spices. Fry to desired crispiness, top with cheese, cover and set aside to allow cheese to melt.

STYLE POINTS: Great with bulgur instead of rice. Use fresh onions and garlic. Serve with tortillas and sour cream dip.

QUICK CURRIED RICE
(SERVES 3–4)

1 cup rice

1 Tbs. onion flakes

1 tsp. curry powder

1 vegetable bouillon cube

2 Tbs. dried red and green peppers

3 cups water

1 cup dried apples, raisins, apricots, cut into small bits

½ cup cashews and/or peanuts

⅓ cup coconut (optional)

HELPFUL HINTS: Bring water, rice, and bouillon cube to a boil. Simmer. When water is half absorbed, add fruit, peppers, and spices. Simmer until done. Mix in nuts, cover with coconut, and serve.

STYLE POINTS: Use couscous instead of rice. When couscous, fruit, and spices are done, fry in oil with nuts. Sprinkle with coconut and serve with chapatis.

FRIED RICE
(SERVES 2–3)

1 cup rice

2 cups water

2 Tbs. onion flakes

2 Tbs. dried red and greed peppers

2 Tbs. soy sauce

¼ tsp. garlic powder

1 Tbs. oil

4 Tbs. egg powder, 1 Tbs. dry milk, and ½ cup water, mixed

Black pepper

Sunflower seeds

HELPFUL HINTS: Cook rice with onion flakes and any vegetables you include. Put oil in frying pan and scramble reconstituted eggs. Add all ingredients and fry until they are thoroughly hot.

STYLE POINTS: Cook 1 package of ramen noodles and fry them with rice. Use garlic tamari instead of soy sauce. Add ½ cup of dried mushrooms and/or ½ cup of dried peas and carrots. Top with cashews.

MEXICAN RICE CASSEROLE
(SERVES 3–4)

1 cup rice or grits

1 cup freeze-dried corn

1–2 Tbs. onion flakes

1–2 cups Cheddar, cut into small bits

⅓ cup dry milk

½ tsp. each chili pepper, salt, and pepper

About 3 cups water

HELPFUL HINTS: Cook rice, water, corn, milk, and spices. Mix all ingredients. Pour into fry-bake pan. Cover and warm over low heat until cheese melts.

STYLE POINTS: Serve with tortillas and sour cream dip. Salsa or hot sauce makes a nice addition as well.

QUICK SWEET-AND-SOUR RICE

(SERVES 3–4)

$1/4$ cup red and green peppers

$1/4$ cup raisins or apricots

$1/4$ cup pineapple chunks

3 Tbs. soy sauce

1 cup rice

3 cups water

3 oz. dried tofu or chicken (optional)

1 pkg. sweet-and-sour mix

HELPFUL HINTS: Pour about 1 cup of hot water over dried tofu/meat, fruit, and peppers. Cook rice with 2 cups water. Add sweet-and-sour mix and soy sauce to fruit and vegetable mix. Return to a boil. Pour over rice. Mix and serve.

STYLE POINTS: Serve with almonds.

RICE AND POTATO PATTIES

1 cup cooked rice

2 cups water

4 Tbs. dry milk

$2/3$ cup instant potatoes

$1/2$ cup cheese, cut into small bits

Garlic powder, salt, and pepper to taste

2 Tbs. margarine

HELPFUL HINTS: Boil $3/4$ cup water with milk and margarine. Remove from heat, add cheese, instant potatoes, rice, and set aside for a couple of minutes. Spice to taste, form into patties, and fry in margarine or oil. (Great use for leftover rice. If you cook it with a couple of instant soups, it's even better.)

STYLE POINTS: Cover with brown gravy. Add a few sunflower seeds.

CHICKEN CURRY
(SERVES 4)

2 oz. freeze-dried chicken

1 pkg. freeze-dried peas

1 env. Knorr Leek Soup

1 env. Herb-Ox Instant Chicken Broth

3–4 tsps. curry powder

1½ cups instant rice

Coconut flakes, cashews, raisins, or dried cranberries

HELPFUL HINTS: Bring 5 to 6 cups of water to a boil. Add chicken, peas, leek soup mix, and chicken broth. Set aside to rehydrate (15 to 30 minutes). Add curry powder. Bring back to a boil and add instant rice. Cook 5 to 10 minutes until tender, stirring occasionally. Sprinkle with coconut, cashews, and raisins and serve.

Thanks to Iretta Hunter, Danville, California.

Pasta

Most outdoor folks we know are addicted to pasta. It's quick, filling, readily available in wonderfully different shapes and colors, and can even be tasty if you cook it right. We've climbed several high peaks on pasta alone, so you can trust us on this: Mac-and-cheese gets old fourteen days straight. You can buy pasta in ready-made dishes. We find they are usually too small and expensive for common outdoor use.

ESSENTIAL PASTA RECIPE
(SERVES 3–4)

3 cups pasta

6 cups water

1 tsp. oil (optional)

OR

1 part pasta to 2 parts water

HELPFUL HINTS: Heat water to a rolling boil, then add oil and pasta. Cook pasta until it is tender. The time can vary a lot. Angelhair and Chinese noodles take a short time (3 to 5 minutes) versus shells and whole-wheat elbows, which take longer (12 to 15 minutes). Fettuccini and spaghetti are somewhere in the middle. Altitude will add to the cooking time, since the water is boiling at a lower temperature. Choose your pastas carefully if you will be traveling above 10,000 feet. Whole-wheat and vegetable pastas require the longest cooking times and often go from still crunchy to glue without ever reaching that "perfect" moment. *Important:* If you add the pasta before the water boils, you are guaranteed to be left with wallpaper paste instead of dinner. Pasta loves company . . . in other words, test pasta frequently to avoid mushy problems.

SERVING SUGGESTIONS: Any of the cream sauces or peanut butter sauces combines well with pasta. (See Sauces for recipes.)

SERVING SIZE: A pound of pasta generally satisfies 4 folks if you're also having soup and bread or dessert. We do know many hardy hikers who can easily consume 8 ounces themselves. On cold, long days of hiking, we (the authors) regularly split a pound of pasta. But on warm desert nights, we get by splitting a half pound. So what's the answer? Play around until you figure it out.

Popular Variations on the Theme

FETTUCCINI ALFREDO
(SERVES 3–4)

1 lb. fettuccini

1¹/₂–2 cups Alfredo Sauce (see Sauces)

Parmesan cheese

HELPFUL HINTS: Make the Alfredo Sauce first and set aside. Cook and drain pasta. Warm sauce, stirring constantly. Add to pasta and serve with Parmesan cheese.

STYLE POINTS: Add hydrated vegetables for a primavera touch, or add seafood you harvested yourself.

ITALIAN SPAGHETTI
(SERVES 3–4)

1 lb. thin spaghetti noodles

1¹/₂–2 cups Italian Tomato Sauce (see Sauces)

Parmesan cheese

HELPFUL HINTS: Prepare Italian Tomato Sauce. Cook and drain pasta. Warm sauce, add to pasta, and serve with Parmesan cheese.

STYLE POINTS: Add lentils, falafel balls, summer sausage, or hydrated beef to your sauce. It's also a good protein boost.

MACARONI AND CHEESE

(SERVES 3–4)

3 cups elbows or shells

1¹/₂–2 cups Mustard Cheese Sauce (see Sauces)

¹/₄ cup sunflower seeds

2 Tbs. onion flakes

HELPFUL HINTS: Prepare the Mustard Cheese Sauce first, adding the onion flakes with the other sauce ingredients. Cook and drain pasta. Add warmed sauce, add seeds, and serve. For quick mac-and-cheese leave about 1 cup of water when draining the noodles, add all ingredients for sauce to the pot, and warm slowly over a low flame.

STYLE POINTS: Add hydrated peas and tuna for a Tuna Casserole Deluxe. Serve with croutons.

ALPINE SPAGHETTI

(SERVE 3–4)

1 lb. thin spaghetti

4 Tbs. oil

1 cup Parmesan cheese

4–6 tsps. ground sweet basil

1–2 Tbs. parsley flakes

Garlic powder and pepper to taste

HELPFUL HINTS: Cook and drain pasta. Add oil and toss, then mix in the remaining ingredients.

Thanks to Kitty Ann and Roger Cox, Pitkin, Colorado.

AMERICAN CHOP SUEY

(SERVES 3–4)

3 cups elbows or shells

2 cups cream of tomato instant soup (2 pkgs.) or

　　2 cups Tomato Cream Sauce (see Sauces)

1–2 Tbs. onion flakes

¹/₄ cup dried red and green peppers (optional)

1 cup dried ground beef or any type of hardy sausage cut into small bits

HELPFUL HINTS: Cook and drain pasta. Add dried ground beef, onion flakes, and dried peppers to 2 cups of water, bring to a boil, and simmer 5 to 10 minutes to hydrate the ingredients. Add tomato soups, mix all ingredients, and serve with black pepper.

HOT RED PEPPER PASTA
(SERVES 2–4)

1 lb. linguini or fettuccini

¼ cup olive oil

2 tsps. minced garlic or garlic powder to taste

1 tsp. crushed red pepper

2 Tbs. parsley flakes

HELPFUL HINTS: Cook and drain pasta. Heat oil and sauté garlic. (Skip this step if using garlic powder.) Add remaining ingredients and toss until pasta is coated. Be careful with the crushed red pepper.

STYLE POINTS: Top with Parmesan and tamari to taste.

SPAGHETTI A LA CARBONDALE
(SERVES 3–4)

1 lb. thin spaghetti

2–3 Tbs. oil

1 Tbs. onion flakes or 1 small onion

2–4 garlic cloves or ¼–½ tsp. garlic powder

2 Tbs. parsley flakes

2 tsps. oregano

2 reconstituted eggs (4 Tbs. egg powder and 4 Tbs. water)

1 cup small bits of cheese (Swiss is nice here)

HELPFUL HINTS: Cook and drain spaghetti. Sauté onion, garlic, oil, and spices until tender. Add all ingredients to cooked spaghetti, stir, and let it sit, covered, for a few minutes so the eggs will cook and cheese will melt.

STYLE POINTS: Add 1 cup of white wine and an 8-ounce can of whole baby clams to the sauce.

MILL VALLEY LINGUINI
(SERVES 3–4)

1 lb. linguini

½ cup dry milk

2 cups water

1 cup sun-dried tomatoes

½ cup dried mushrooms

Parmesan cheese

HELPFUL HINTS: Cut tomatoes and mushrooms into smaller pieces and cover with hot water to hydrate them. Cook and drain pasta. Add milk and water and bring to a boil. Add the vegetables and whatever liquid is left. Simmer for several minutes. Add sauce to pasta. Sprinkle with Parmesan cheese and pepper.

HOT OR COLD "SZECHWAN" NOODLES
(SERVES 4–5)

1 lb. spaghetti- or linguini-type noodles

1 1/2 cup Sesame-Peanut Sauce (see Sauces)

HELPFUL HINTS: Cook and drain pasta. Prepare Hot Sesame-Peanut Sauce and stir into pasta. If you don't like hot foods or aren't carrying sesame oil, this is very tasty with Peanut Butter Gravy.

STYLE POINTS: Top with scallions. For the truly brave, add cayenne.

Truly Gourmet

LISAGNA LASAGNA
(SERVES 3–4)

1/2 cup wheat flour

1/2 cup white flour

1 1/4 cups water

2 cups pasta (elbows, shells spirals, etc.)

1 Tbs. baking powder (adjust for the altitude; see Backcountry Baking)

2 Tbs. powdered milk

2 Tbs. powdered egg

1 cup Italian Tomato Sauce (see Sauces)

1/4 lb. sliced cheese

4 garlic cloves

1/2 onion

1 Tbs. oil

Oregano

HELPFUL HINTS: Cook pasta. Sauté onion and garlic in oil. Remove from pan. In a separate pan mix flours, dry milk, egg powder, baking powder, and water. Mixture should be the consistency of pancake batter. Put noodles in the bottom of the fry-bake pan and pour batter over the top. Make sauce, substituting fresh sautéed onion and garlic for recommended dry ingredients. Spread sauce over top of mixture in the pan. Cover with thin slices of cheese. Sprinkle with oregano. Stove-top bake for 20 minutes.

Thanks to Lisa Jaeger of Wyoming, Baja, Chile, Alaska, et cetera. She keeps threatening to stay in one place, but we don't believe her.

SMOKED SALMON PASTA
(SERVES 4)

4 garlic cloves

2 shallots

3 Tbs. butter

4 Tbs. dried tomato bits

1 env. Herb-Ox Instant Chicken Broth

8 oz. dry, smoked salmon

8 oz. angelhair pasta

¼ cup capers

Parmesan cheese

HELPFUL HINTS: Peel and chop garlic cloves and shallots in butter. Add dried tomato bits, chicken broth, and ½ cup water. Let sit 15 to 20 minutes. Flake salmon into garlic-tomato mix. Cook noodles and drain. Toss noodles, salmon-garlic-tomato mix, and capers. Serve sprinkled with Parmesan cheese.

Thanks to Iretta Hunter, Danville, California.

HOT TOFU AND SESAME NOODLES
(SERVES 4)

3 pkgs. ramen noodles

1½ cups Hot Sesame-Peanut Sauce (see Sauces)

⅓ cup sesame seeds

½ cup peanuts or cashews

½ pound tofu or 3 oz. dried tofu

HELPFUL HINTS: Soften dried tofu by soaking in hot water for about 10 minutes. Prepare Hot Sesame-Peanut Sauce. Cook and drain ramen. Do not use flavoring packet. Combine all ingredients except peanuts/cashews. Smash these up and sprinkle them on just before serving.

STYLE POINTS: Garnish with green onions or sprouts.

VEGETABLE AND SHRIMP PASTA

(SERVES 2–4)

$^1/_2$ cup oil

1 lb. shrimp (fresh or canned)

2 garlic cloves or $^1/_4$ tsp. garlic powder

2 cups water

1 pkg. Knorr Vegetable Soup and Recipe Mix or equivalent

1 tsp. oregano

$^1/_4$ tsp. crushed red pepper

8 oz. linguini

HELPFUL HINTS: If using fresh shrimp, sauté shrimp and garlic in oil until shrimp turn pink (about 5 minutes). Remove them from pan. Add water, soup mix, oregano, and red pepper to frying pan and bring to a boil. Simmer for 5 to 10 minutes. Return shrimp to pan (or add canned shrimp). Warm and spoon over cooked and drained pasta.

STYLE POINTS: Use fresh shrimp. Substitute 1 cup of white wine for 1 cup of water. Works well with clams or mussels as well.

Potatoes

Harvested as early as 6000 B.C. by South American Indians, this staple of the Incan Empire and the Irish was brought to the United States in the early eighteenth century. Its popularity soared around the turn of the century, and then plummeted again in the 1950s. Currently, potatoes are on the upswing, but it's mostly in the french-fried form. Potatoes are a nutritious, hardy addition to a backcountry menu. Unfortunately, their bulk and weight turn most folks to the dried or flake options. If you can afford the space and need the weight, fresh potatoes will be tastier and healthier. They make a great addition to base camp or waterborne travel where weight is less of a consideration. If nothing else, they make a great first breakfast before you hit the trail. Dehydrated potato flakes, granules, and hash browns are widely available at supermarkets. Additionally, many companies are marketing dehydrated potato and sauce mixes. Watch out for these—many are very high in fat and sodium. If you choose to buy them for the variety or ease of preparation, carefully consult the box for serving size information. A cup and a half per person is reasonable.

ESSENTIAL INSTANT POTATO FLAKES
(OR PEARLS)
(SERVES 1)

⅔ cup potato flakes

2–3 Tbs. dry milk

1 glob margarine

Salt and pepper to taste

⅔ cup hot water

HELPFUL HINTS: Heat water, milk, and margarine. Stir in potatoes until just moist. Let stand for 30 to 60 seconds. Add spices and eat.

SERVING SUGGESTIONS: Instant potato flakes or pearls are invaluable backcountry menu additions. They are an especially quick breakfast or snack before dinner, can be fried up for any meal, and make a great thickener when you put too much water in your soup. They are not good in coffee, so when you wake up gummy eyed in the morning, don't mistake them for powdered milk.

STYLE POINTS: Reconstitute potatoes with a cup of instant soup. Add chunked cheese, garlic, and chili pepper.

Popular Variations on the Theme

POTATO-NUT PATTIES

2 cups potatoes (follow the above recipe to hydrate)

2 cups chopped nuts (we like walnuts)

⅓ cup melted margarine

1 Tbs. onion or chives

1 Tbs. parsley flakes

HELPFUL HINTS: Mix all ingredients together. Form into patties. Fry in oil over medium heat. You can make them without the nuts.

STYLE POINTS: Top with cheese. Melt and serve.

CHEESY POTATO CASSEROLE
(SERVES 2–4)

6 oz. dried hash browns or sliced potatoes

1 ⅓ cups water

1 cup Mustard Cheese Sauce (see Sauces)

HELPFUL HINTS: Bring water to a boil. Add potatoes and simmer until tender. Make Mustard Cheese Sauce in fry-bake pan. Add potatoes, mix, and bake for 15 minutes or so.

STYLE POINTS: Top with chives and sour cream.

Truly Gourmet

SPICY SHEPHERD'S PIE
(SERVES 4–6)

1 ½–2 cups instant refried bean (or black bean) mix

2 cups instant potatoes

2 Tbs. onion flakes

1 bouillon cube or instant soup

⅓ cup dry milk

3 Tbs. margarine

1 cup freeze-dried corn

1 cup cheese, cut into small bits

Salt, pepper, and Tabasco to taste

HELPFUL HINTS: Combine 2 cups of hot water with potatoes, milk, margarine, and bouillon cube. Set aside. In the bottom of your fry-bake pan, combine 2 to 3 cups of boiling water with corn, instant potatoes, onion flakes, and beans. Simmer until corn is tender and beans hydrated. Remove from heat. Spread potatoes over beans; add salt, pepper, and Tabasco. Top with cheese. Stove-top bake until hot and cheese melts (about 15 minutes).

STYLE POINTS: Substitute 1 cup of dried ground beef or sausage for half of the beans. Top with sour cream.

GRAPE-NUT SURPRISE
(aka POWER LOAD DINNER)
(SERVES 3–4)

2 cups potato flakes

2 cups instant refried beans

2 cups Cheddar cheese

2 cups Grape-Nuts

¼ cup margarine

Black pepper, chili pepper, cayenne, garlic powder to taste

HELPFUL HINTS: Boil 2 pots of water with 2 cups of water in each. Hydrate potato flakes and refried beans in separate pots. Mix chili pepper, pepper, and cayenne into beans to taste. Be careful if you bought refrieds that already have been spiced. Set both aside. Melt margarine in bottom of fry-bake pan. Add two thirds of the Grape-Nuts until they are saturated with fat. Remove from heat and smash into a crust. Cover crust with a layer of sliced Cheddar. Add a layer of potatoes and a layer of beans. Top with a final layer of cheese and sprinkle with Grape-Nuts, garlic, and chili powder. Stove-top bake until the cheese has melted (about 10 to 15 minutes).

Thanks to Shana Tarter and Steve Platz, Pitkin, Colorado. They needed this on their honeymoon.

SIMPLE POTATO CURRY
(SERVES 2)

2 cups dried hash brown potatoes

1⅓ cups water

2–3 Tbs. margarine

1–2 tsps. curry powder

½ tsp. garlic powder

HELPFUL HINTS: Fry all ingredients together until water is absorbed and potatoes are tender.

STYLE POINTS: Top with sour cream.

Beans: The Musical Fruit

Actually, beans aren't fruit at all. They're all dried seeds from leguminous plants. Each bean (legume) has a characteristic flavor and texture, and all beans are excellent sources of protein when combined with grains, seeds, or small amounts of milk, cheese, or meat. The problem with beans in the backcountry is not the snide remarks from your traveling companions but the time they take to cook. A pot of legumes can take from twenty minutes (lentils) to three and a half hours (chickpeas) to soften to the point that they are edible. Don't let this discourage you; just choose carefully. Lentils and split peas make wonderful backcountry meals, and many beans, such as pintos and black beans, can be purchased in quick-cooking styles. Soaking and pressure-cooking beans can cut down on the cooking time as well. And don't forget that falafel and NatureBurger are also bean by-products. Bean dishes are widely available in prepackaged forms from supermarkets, health food stores, and outdoor retailers. Below are some dishes you can easily throw together yourself.

ESSENTIAL LENTILS
(SERVES 2)

1 cup lentils

3 cups water

1/4 tsp. salt

HELPFUL HINTS: Cover lentils with water and bring to a boil. Cover and simmer for 20 to 40 minutes until tender. Although presoaking is not required, we find it cuts down of the cooking time. Carry them soaking in a water bottle while you hike or paddle.

SERVING SUGGESTIONS: Top with Curry Sauce (see Sauces).

ESSENTIAL INSTANT REFRIED BEANS OR BLACK BEANS
(SERVES 2)

1 cup instant beans

3/4–1 cup water

1–2 Tbs. margarine

HELPFUL HINTS: If you have bean flakes, you can add the margarine and boiling water to beans and set aside while they hydrate (5 to 10 minutes). At high altitude or if you have dried whole beans, some limited simmering may be required. If your beans are not prespiced, add salt, pepper, chili powder, and cumin to taste.

SERVING SUGGESTIONS: Top with cheese and use a tortilla as a spoon.

STYLE POINTS: Serve with sour cream and sprouts.

ESSENTIAL FALAFEL
(SERVES 2)

1 cup falafel
3/4 cup water
Oil for frying

HELPFUL HINTS: Mix falafel with water and let stand. Form into thin patties (½ inch) and fry in oil. Don't squish them with the spatula while they're in the pan or they will break apart. This is fragile business.

SERVING SUGGESTIONS: Top with a slice of cheese, roll in a tortilla, sprinkle on the Tabasco, and eat. Falafel burgers are also delicious with many of this book's sauces (see Sauces).

STYLE POINTS: Form into meatball-sized rounds and serve with Italian spaghetti. We call this spaghetti and falafel balls.

Popular Variations on the Bean Theme

LENTIL CHILI
(SERVES 3–4)

1½ cups lentils
4–5 cups water
4 Tbs. tomato powder
1–2 Tbs. onion flakes
1 Tbs. chili powder, or more to taste
1 tsp. cumin
1 tsp. oregano
1 tsp. garlic powder
2 Tbs. cornmeal
Black and red pepper to taste
Cheddar cheese

HELPFUL HINTS: Combine water and lentils and bring to a boil. Add all ingredients (except cheese) and simmer until done. Serve and top with cheese chunks.

STYLE POINTS: Add dried peppers, corn, or tomatoes to the chili. Serve over corn bread.

CURRIED LENTILS
(SERVES 3–4)

1 cup lentils

3 cups water

1–2 Tbs. onion flakes

1–2 tsps. curry powder

1 vegetable bouillon cube

1 cup chopped dried fruit

$^1\!/_2$ cup sunflower seeds or other suitable nuts

$^1\!/_3$ cup coconut (optional)

HELPFUL HINTS: Bring water, lentils, and bouillon cube to a boil. When water is half absorbed, add fruit and spices. Simmer until lentils are tender. Add nuts and coconut and serve.

STYLE POINTS: Use a mixture of lentils and rice, or bulgur and rice.

LENTIL PILAF
(SERVES 3–4)

$^1\!/_2$ cup lentils

$^1\!/_2$ cup rice

$2^1\!/_2$–3 cups water

1–2 pkgs. instant soup (cream of chicken or tomato works well)

1 cup dried carrots

2 Tbs. margarine

4–6 Tbs. dried red and green peppers

2 Tbs. onion flakes

1 tsp. cumin

$^1\!/_2$ tsp. basil

$^1\!/_2$ tsp. garlic powder

HELPFUL HINTS: Boil water, add all ingredients, and simmer until tender.

STYLE POINTS: After everything is tender, fry the pilaf in margarine. Top it with cheese and nuts. Melt and serve.

SWEET-AND-SOUR LENTILS

(SERVES 3–4)

1 cup lentils

3 cups water

¼ cup red and green peppers

¼ cup raisins

¼ cup pineapple chunks or chopped apricots

3 Tbs. soy sauce

¼ cup dried carrots

1 pkg. sweet-and-sour mix

HELPFUL HINTS: Pour hot water over dried fruit and vegetables. Cook lentils. Add package and soy sauce to fruit and vegetable mix, and return to a boil. Pour over lentils, mix, and serve.

STYLE POINTS: Serve with almonds or combine with pasta for a larger group.

LENTIL PATTIES

(SERVES 3–4)

1 cup lentils

1 cup bulgur

3–4 cups water

½ tsp. garlic powder

1 Tbs. parsley flakes

1 Tbs. onion flakes

2 Tbs. oil

¼ tsp. black pepper

¼ cup flour

HELPFUL HINTS: Combine onions, garlic, lentils, and 3 to 4 cups of water. Simmer for 20 to 25 minutes. Add bulgur, parsley, oil, and spices. Simmer until tender. Mash and mix in flour. If for some reason the mixture is too thin to form patties, add more flour or cornmeal. Form into patties; crisp in buttered frying pan.

STYLE POINTS: Serve topped with Peanut Sauce (see Sauces).

Truly Gourmet

ENCHILADA PIE

(SERVES 4)

3 10-inch (or the size of your baking pan) flour tortillas

2 cups dried instant refried beans

1½ cups Mexican Sauce (see Sauces)

¼ cup red and green peppers

1 cup dried corn

2 cups cheese, cut into slices

1 package sour cream mix

HELPFUL HINTS: Add 2½ to 3 cups of boiling water to beans and vegetables. Cover and set aside. Put together the sauce. Pour a third of sauce in the bottom of deep-dish frying pan. Alternate 3 layers of tortillas, beans, and cheese. Spread remaining sauce on top. Stove-top bake for 20 to 30 minutes. Top with sour cream and serve.

Pizza

(SERVES 2)

Pizza is a quick and easy dinner that consistently amazes your friends and, sometimes, even your enemies. All you need is a deep-dish frying pan with a lid and the courage to try. Below you will find some crusts of varying intensity of commitment, plus some traditional and not-so-traditional toppings.

Bottoms

(THESE CRUSTS FIT A 9- TO 10-INCH DEEP-DISH PAN)

SUPERQUICK CRUST

If you have a low commitment level, for the quickest pizzalike meal, heat your frying pan and one side of a tortilla or pita bread, flip it over, add the toppings and the lid until the cheese melts, and you're eating a pizzalike treat in less than 10 minutes.

QUICK PIZZA CRUST

¾ cup Essential Batter Mix (see Backcountry Baking)

¾ cup flour

½ cup water

1 Tbs. oil

HELPFUL HINTS: Mix into a stiff dough. Oil bottom of fry-bake pan. Press dough firmly into bottom of pan. For a low commitment level, flip-bake the crust about 10 minutes a side. (Add toppings after the flip!) If you have the time, add toppings and stove-top bake for higher style points.

STYLE POINTS: Add 1 to 2 teaspoons of Italian seasoning to the dough before mixing in the water.

THE "REAL THING" PIZZA CRUST

1 Tbs. dry yeast

1 Tbs. sugar or honey

¼ tsp. salt

1½ cups flour

⅔–¾ cup lukewarm water

HELPFUL HINTS: Combine yeast, sugar, and water in an insulated mug. When yeast froths to the top, combine slowly with flour and salt, stirring at first and then kneading until the dough is smooth. Put in a warm place to double in size. Knead again until dough is smooth. Press into bottom of oiled pan, add toppings, and stove-top bake about 20 to 30 minutes.

(For more help on yeast and baking in general, see Backcountry Baking.)

Tops

TRADITIONAL LID

¾ cup Italian Tomato Sauce (see Sauces)

1 cup Mozzarella cheese

Veggies of your choice

Parmesan cheese

HELPFUL HINTS: Top crust of your choice with sauce, hydrated vegetables, and cheese. Bake by preferred method.

HERB LID

1 cup Cheese Sauce (see Sauces)

½–1 Tbs. basil, chives, sage, or rosemary (or a combination)

HELPFUL HINTS: Top crust of your choice and bake by preferred method.

MEAT LOVER'S LID

1 cup Italian Tomato Sauce

OR

1 cup Tomato Cream Sauce (see Sauces)

1 cup cheese, cut into small bits

1 cup sliced sausage or pepperoni

HELPFUL HINTS: Top crust of your choice with sauce, meat, and finally cheese. Bake by preferred method.

VEGETARIAN LID

1 cup Italian Tomato Sauce (see Sauces)

1–2 cups dried vegetables (peppers and mushrooms work well)

1 cup cheese, cut into small bits

HELPFUL HINTS: Top crust of your choice with sauce, hydrated vegetables, and cheese. Bake by preferred method.

STYLE POINTS: Substitute tomato sauce for cream sauce. Sprinkle with sunflower seeds.

TRUSTAFERRIAN LID

1 cup Alfredo Sauce (see Sauces)

1 cup dried mushrooms

1 cup sun-dried tomatoes

Parmesan cheese and crushed red pepper to taste

HELPFUL HINTS: Top your crust of choice with sauce, hydrated mushrooms, and tomatoes. Bake by preferred method. Let folks sprinkle the Parmesan and, especially, the red pepper themselves . . . if you like them.

STYLE POINTS: Top with sprouts.

HOT TO TROT LID

1 cup Mexican Sauce (see Sauces)

1 cup freeze-dried corn

1 cup Cheddar cheese, cut into small bits

Tabasco to taste

HELPFUL HINTS: Top crust of your choice with sauce, hydrated corn, and cheese. (Goes well with Pan Corn Bread; see Backcountry Baking.) Bake by preferred method.

STYLE POINTS: Add 1 cup of meat, lentils, or beans to sauce.

Fresh Fish

Let's say, for the sake of a poetic moment, that trout—name your preferred species: rainbows, cutthroats, browns—are rising to dry flies on a splendid mountain lake. You've landed a couple that will just about fit in the pan you're carrying. Dinner awaits.

Clean the fish soon after catching. Slit the abdomen open from vent to chin, slice off the head, and remove the entrails. Scrape out the kidney tissue that lies along the backbone within the body cavity. This stuff comes off easily with your thumbnail as a tool. Wash what remains of the fish thoroughly in cold water.

If it's a trout, the cleaning is finished. Scaly fish, such as a south Georgia sunfish, will need the scales removed before cooking. Lay a scaly fish on its side and, with the dull side of a knife blade, remove the scales by scraping from tail to neck with brisk little strokes. The sooner after deciding the fish will be eaten you undertake the scaling operation, the smoother the operation will go.

FRIED FISH

Fish (any species is suitable for frying)

Butter

Flour or cornmeal

Spices: salt, pepper, Mrs. Dash

HELPFUL HINTS: If the butter is warm enough, rub a bit on the fish first. Sprinkle on the spices. Liberally coat the fish with flour or cornmeal. Obviously, you can fry fish without flour or cornmeal, but they seal in and add to the fish's flavor. Melt a little butter in a pan, and plop in the fish. Watch it carefully. As soon as the flesh is no longer translucent, turn the fish over with a spatula, and continue the careful watching, removing as soon as the flesh lifts easily from the bone. *Caution:* It is very easy to overcook and, therefore, ruin a fish. Err toward undercooking for the best bet in fried fish.

POACHED FISH

Fish (leaner fish lend themselves better to poaching)
Salt

HELPFUL HINTS: Thoroughly salt the fish and place it in a pan. Add water to the pan until the fish is barely covered. Put a lid on the pan and bring the water to a boil. Reduce the heat to a simmer and cook until the flesh is flaky, usually about 10 minutes.

STYLE POINTS: Add onion powder, or (better) onion flakes, or (even better) a chopped onion to the water.

FISH CHOWDER

(Serves 2)

Fish, cut into small chunks (fatter fish work better)
1 cup dehydrated hash brown potatoes
¼ cup onion flakes
1 Tbs. green pepper flakes (if available)
Powdered milk (enough to make 1 quart when reconstituted)
Potato Buds
Salt and pepper
Optional: a handful of dried mushrooms, corn, peas, or whatever you have
  that looks like a vegetable

HELPFUL HINTS: Put the hash browns, onion, pepper flakes, vegetables, and milk in a pot, and mix with enough water to rehydrate the stuff and make a slushy soup. Bring it to a boil, stirring frequently, then add enough Potato Buds to thicken the chowder to the consistency you like. Add more water if it gets too thick. Add salt and pepper to taste.

Once the chowder is cooked to your liking, reduce the heat to a light boil and throw in chunks of raw fish. Cook for 5 more minutes. Time it so you don't overcook the fish. Serve hot.

Thanks to Cliff Jacobson, River Falls, Wisconsin.

Backcountry Baking

urely this was a dream. Breakfast deep in the backcountry takes on an unappealing familiarity: cold granola, sticky oatmeal, something unidentifiable dumped into lukewarm water in hopes it will dissolve completely before you try to swallow it. But this cold Wind River morning, waiting for the sun to crawl over the ridge before I crawled out of the bag, friendly aromas sat me up under the sheltering tarp. There was fresh coffee and, yes, the warm smell of baking yeast and . . . what was it?

She looked up from the whispering stove and smiled. "Let's go. Cinnamon rolls are almost ready."

Served hot, the melting butter dribbled over my fingers. "Great! Wonderful! Terrific!" I searched futilely for descriptives, knowing I had found a backpacking partner I didn't want to lose. That was over a decade ago, and we're still baking together. The longer the trip, the more we appreciate these freshly baked changes in diet.

Option 1: Stove-Top Baking

The Tools

You will need one deep (1½ to 2 inches) nonstick fry-bake pan with a lid that fits snugly. Your batter or dough should not overfill the pan. Half full is a good gauge, or the rising that ensues when you bake will cause the batter to overflow or minimally stick to the lid. The lid must fit tightly to ensure that you adequately trap the required amount of heat. If your pan is smaller than this, merely cut the recipes in half and proceed as directed. We like the large pan even for the two of us because if you are going to the trouble to bake, it's rewarding to have leftovers. Okay, we're pigs.

The Heat

You will need a source of bottom heat—in this case, a backpacking stove that simmers well. In preparation for stove-top baking, light your chosen stove and adjust it to a simmer. You should be able to hold your hand comfortably about 10 inches above the stove, but still feel your hand being warmed. Too hot is generally more of a problem than too cold.

Equally as important as bottom heat is a source of top heat. Traditionally, this is where you build a small, hot, twiggy fire on top of your lid. We have discovered the convection dome marketed by Backpacker's Pantry as a better alternative. We will discuss both options.

Stove-top Baking with the Twiggy Fire

Gather a pile of pencil-sized or smaller twigs. Light your stove and let it run at its lowest heat. Put the baking pan, with secure lid, on the stove, and build a twiggy fire on the lid. Spread the fire out evenly on the lid, and feed it enough wood to keep it burning. It's almost impossible to produce too much heat on the lid. Every four to five minutes, rotate the pan clockwise to assure even baking on the bottom. Use a couple of sticks to make rotating the pan simple and painless. Total cooking time usually runs thirty to forty minutes. After twenty to thirty minutes, or if you start to smell the rich aroma, carefully lift off the lid and check the progress, just to be safe. *Don't lift the lid too often,* or you will keep losing the heat needed to bake the goodie. When the dough is cooked, it has a firm crust and sounds hollow when you thump it. Set the pan off the stove, but continue to burn the twiggy fire on top until nothing is left except a fine ash that can be scattered harmlessly.

Stove-top Baking with Convection Dome

This item has revolutionized our stove-top baking. Follow the directions for baking with a twiggy fire, only skip the twiggies. The convection dome surrounds the fry-bake pan, trapping all the heat around and on top of the pan. You have a lightweight mini oven! Although the twiggy fire works great, the convection dome cuts down on baking time (about 30 percent), and the chance of fire. It folds neatly into the pan for travel. We love it and go nowhere without it. (Okay, maybe a couple of places.) Basically, what you're doing is converting your pan into the Outback Oven (see Gear for the Outdoor Kitchen).

Option 2: Flip-Baking

Flip-baking is faster. You end up with a still tasty yet denser version of your stove-top baked bread. It is useful if you are in a rush, you forgot your convection dome (heaven forbid), the twiggy supply in the area is low, or the fire danger is high. Merely oil your fry-bake pan, place the dough or batter inside, and flip carefully when it is done on one side. Cook until both sides are toasty and the middle is not gooey. Time per side depends on thickness of the dough and the heat of the stove. To prevent "black on the outside, goo on the inside," flip-bake over medium heat with the lid in place. We traditionally flip-bake pancakes, pan biscuits, chapatis, tortillas, johnnycakes, and many other things when we're too hungry to wait.

ESSENTIAL BATTER MIX

The initial Essential Batter Mix ingredients will vary from pancakes to quick breads to piecrust. What will vary is the consistency of the batter and the additional ingredients (the ingredients that make it special). For example, pancake batter needs to be lumpless and pour easily; muffins and cakes need to be thicker but still pour if you encourage it; and biscuit dough needs to be just that, dough (sticky, but you can form it into a ball and it stays there). So these recipes will include some ideas about amounts of fluid needed, but the best plan is to add water slowly until the batter is the desired consistency.

B2's ESSENTIAL BATTER MIX

2 cups flour

$^1/_3$–$^1/_2$ cup dry milk

4 tsps. baking powder

$^1/_2$ cup margarine or shortening

$^1/_2$ tsp. salt (optional)

Water

HOW MUCH WATER?

For pancake batter: About 2 cups. Batter should run off spoon easily.

For cake batter: About 1$^1/_2$ to 1$^3/_4$ cups. Batter should walk off spoon quickly.

For muffin/quick bread batter: About 1$^1/_4$ to 1$^1/_2$ cups. Batter should drop off spoon into pan, but it's not in a huge rush. This batter is about twice as thick as pancakes.

For biscuit batter: About $^3/_4$ cup. This batter is quite stiff but still sticky. You definitely have to push it off the spoon or press it into a pan. It will not go anywhere by itself.

Important: Altitude Adjustments!

The thing that does seriously affect baking is the altitude at which you are cooking. The higher you go, the less leavening agent (baking powder) you will need. So when making your Essential Batter Mix, either at home or on the trail, think about your altitude and adjust your ingredients appropriately. Also, buy double-acting baking powder. It releases its leavening in two stages so cakes won't rise too fast.

If you do not adjust for the altitude, your baked goods will expand out of your pan, crumble into a small pile, and be otherwise inedible without rolling them into crumb balls or eating them with a spoon.

BAKING POWDER: Use double-acting.

0–3,500 feet: Use 4 tsp. per 2 cups flour.

3,500–6,500: se 3½ tsp. per 2 cups flour.

6,500–8,500: Use 3 tsp. per 2 cups of flour.

8,500–10,000: Use 2½ tsp. per 2 cups of flour.

Over 10,000: Use 2 tsp. and an extra egg (2 Tbs. powdered egg) per 2 cups of flour.

There are more exact adjustments, but this works. If the recipe calls for a lot of sugar, many people cut it back a tablespoon or two as they gain elevation. We don't usually worry about it, but using too much sugar at the higher altitudes may make your cakes fall by destroying their cell structure.

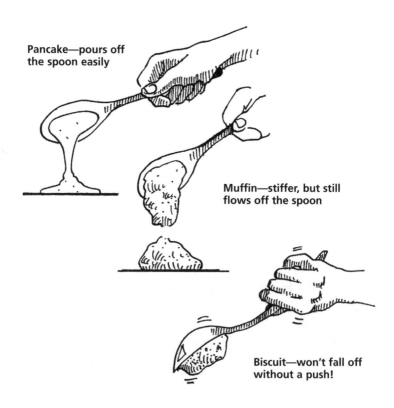

Pancake—pours off the spoon easily

Muffin—stiffer, but still flows off the spoon

Biscuit—won't fall off without a push!

Commercial Mixes

Commercial mixes are prepared for sea level, in fact most have altitude adjustments on the packaging. We found this out when we built our cabin at 9,200 feet. Your cake mixes expand like a bad horror movie all over the oven. To combat this dilemma, you must add extra flour to the mixes. Also, add some extra water to compensate for the extra flour and the fact that water evaporates faster at these drier heights. Please don't be overwhelmed. Use the guidelines below to adjust your commercial mixes before baking.

For every 2 cups of mix add:

3,500–6,500 feet: 2 Tbs. each flour and water.

6,500–8,500: 3 Tbs. each flour and water.

8,500–10,000: 4 Tbs. ($\frac{1}{4}$ cup) each flour and water.

Above 10,000: 4 Tbs. ($\frac{1}{4}$ cup) each flour and water and an extra egg.

ESSENTIAL PAN BISCUITS

2 cups Essential Batter Mix

$\frac{3}{4}$ cup water

HELPFUL HINTS: Mix wet with dry ingredients. Form into a ball. Knead lightly (about 30 seconds). Pinch off balls of dough and form into patties ($\frac{1}{2}$-inch thick) and fry in buttered frying pan a few minutes a side.

STYLE POINTS: Serve smothered in syrup or gravy (see Breakfasts and/or Sauces).

Thanks to Ardath Drown Gray and Elsie Emmons Cummings, who had the courage to teach a small girl how to make biscuits and let her practice. "Cut the shortening with your hands. It's the only way they come out right."

Popular Variations on the Theme

BUTTERMILK BISCUITS: Make the Essential Batter with buttermilk powder and proceed as in Pan Biscuits.

BACON BISCUITS: Add $\frac{1}{3}$ cup bacon bits to Essential Pan Biscuits and proceed as above.

CHEESE AND GARLIC BISCUITS: Add $\frac{1}{2}$ cup grated cheese and $\frac{1}{2}$ tsp. garlic powder to Essential Pan Biscuits.

HERB BISCUITS: Add $\frac{1}{2}$ tsp. dry mustard, $\frac{1}{2}$ tsp. sage, and $1\frac{1}{4}$ tsps. caraway seeds to Essential Pan Biscuits. Other herbs work well, too.

SIN-A-MON BISCUITS: See Breakfasts.

PSEUDOSCONES: See Breakfasts.

Truly Gourmet

TILTON'S TRAVELING OAT CAKES

2 ¼ *cups white flour*

1 *cup wheat flour*

¾ *cup oatmeal*

1 *tsp. salt*

½ *cup sugar*

2 *tsp. baking powder*

2 *Tbs. dry milk*

1 *tsp. cinnamon*

½ *cup oil*

About 1 cup water

HELPFUL HINTS: Bring oil, sugar, dry milk, and water to a boil. Stir until sugar is dissolved and remove from heat. Combine dry ingredients, add sugary milk mixture, and stir until all ingredients are moist. Shape dough into round biscuits ½ inch thick and 3 inches in diameter, and flip-bake as described in Essential Pan Biscuits.

STYLE POINTS: Pull these out at lunch and serve with cheese, jam, or peanut butter.

JAM JEWELS

2 *cups Essential Batter Mix*

¾ *cup water*

Jam or Wild Berry Syrup (see Breakfasts)

HELPFUL HINTS: Follow mixing directions for Essential Pan Biscuits. Form dough into patties approximately 3 inches in diameter and ¼ inch thick. Drop a spoonful of jelly or thick Berry Syrup in the middle. Fold over and pinch edges tightly shut. If you have trouble sealing dough, dab a little water on the edge. Flip-bake in margarine, or snuggle them into the bottom of your pan and stove-top bake.

Quick Breads

SPEEDY BANNOCK:
A Simple Mountain Bread
(MAKES ONE 10-INCH ROUND)

2 cups Essential Batter Mix (we like ½ white, ½ wheat)

1 cup water

HELPFUL HINTS: Mix dry with wet ingredients. Place or press in oiled fry-bake pan. Stove-top or flip-bake until done.

STYLE POINTS: Add cinnamon, sugar, and raisins.

HERB AND CHEESE QUICK BREAD

1 batch Speedy Bannock batter

1 tsp. garlic powder

1 tsp. basil or oregano or Italian spices

¼ cup Parmesan or Romano cheese

HELPFUL HINTS: Combine all ingredients and proceed as in Speedy Bannock.

CORN BREAD
(MAKES ONE 10-INCH ROUND)

1 cup cornmeal

1 cup flour

½ tsp. salt (optional)

1 Tbs. sugar

2 Tbs. egg powder

2 tsps. baking powder

1 Tbs. oil or melted margarine

¼ cup buttermilk powder

1⅓ cups water

HELPFUL HINTS: Combine all ingredients until they are just wet. For traditional johnnycakes, divide the batter into 2 to 3 portions and flip-bake in a frying pan. For corn bread, stove-top bake.

STYLE POINTS: Add 1 cup of hydrated corn and/or 1 cup of cheese bits. For crunchy corn bread, add ¼ cup of sunflower seeds to the batter.

HUSH PUPPIES

1 cup cornmeal

½ cup white flour

1 Tbs. sugar

2½ tsps. baking powder

2 Tbs. egg powder

1 Tbs. onion flakes

3 Tbs. buttermilk powder

Salt to taste

About ¾ cup water

HELPFUL HINTS: Mix all ingredients together thoroughly. Put a liberal amount of oil into a frying pan. Drop by spoonfuls (or shape into patties) into hot oil and fry until they are brown. These are traditionally deep-fried, but you can get away with a lot less oil by turning them frequently.

CHAPATIS
(MAKES 12)

2 cups whole-wheat flour

¾ cup water

½ tsp. salt (optional)

2 Tbs. oil

HELPFUL HINTS: Mix all ingredients and knead until dough is smooth. Pinch off about 12 small balls of equal size. Pat balls into thin patties between your hands until they are very thin. Drop the flattened dough into a hot frying pan. Cook on one side until brown and flip. Cook second side. About 2 minutes a side.

FLOUR TORTILLAS
(MAKES 12)

2 cups white flour

1½ Tbs. shortening or margarine

1 tsp. baking powder

¾ cup cold water

½ tsp. salt (optional)

HELPFUL HINTS: Mix dry ingredients and cut in margarine with a spoon. (We usually blend it with our washed hands.) Add the water slowly until you have a stiff dough. Divide the dough into 12 balls. Roll them out very thin between 2 plastic bags. Use your water bottle as a rolling pin. Flip-bake about 2 minutes a side.

QUICK SWEET BREAD

2 cups Essential Batter Mix

¼–½ cup sugar

2 Tbs. egg powder

1½ cups water

HELPFUL HINTS: Combine dry ingredients and stir in wet. Do not overmix. Pour into oiled fry-bake pan and stove-top bake until done, about 20 to 30 minutes.

Popular Variations on the Theme

FRUIT SWEET BREAD

Add 1 cup of chopped dried fruit (we like apples and raisins, but mixed fruit works well, or just raisins) and ½ teaspoon of cinnamon to the Quick Sweet Bread recipe above. Hydrate fruit with hot water before adding it to mixture.

WILD BERRY BREAD

Add 1 cup of wild berries and proceed as above.

OATMEAL QUICK BREAD

Substitute 1 cup of oats for 1 cup of Basic Batter Mix. Add ½ cup or raisins and ½ teaspoon of cinnamon.

COFFEE CAKES: See Breakfasts.

Truly Gourmet

APRICOT BREAD

1 1/2 *cups Essential Batter Mix*

1/2 *cup Grape-Nuts*

2/3 *cup dried chopped apricots*

1/2 *cup sugar*

2 *Tbs. egg powder*

1 1/4–1 1/2 *cups water*

HELPFUL HINTS: Pour boiling water over the apricots. Combine all dry ingredients and mix in wet. Add hydrated apricots. Pour into oiled fry-bake pan and stove-top bake until done, about 20 to 30 minutes.

STYLE POINTS: Add 1/2 cup chopped nuts. Pecans are nice.

BACKCOUNTRY CARROT BREAD

2 *cups Essential Batter Mix or any commercial baking mix*

1/2 *cup dry milk*

1/2 *cup brown sugar*

1 *tsp. cinnamon*

1 *grated carrot*

1 *handful of raisins*

3/4–1 *cup water*

HELPFUL HINTS: Combine batter mix, dry milk, sugar, and cinnamon. Gently add carrot, raisins, and water. Mix until all ingredients are wet, and press into the bottom of fry-bake pan. Flip-bake on low heat until done.

Thanks to J. Scott McGee, Redmond, Oregon.

PEANUT BUTTER BREAD

2 *cups flour*

4 *tsps. baking powder*

1/3 *cup sugar*

3/4 *cup peanut butter*

1/2 *cup dry milk*

2 *Tbs. egg powder*

1 1/3 *cups water*

HELPFUL HINTS: Combine all dry ingredients. Cut in peanut butter with 2 knives or forks until the mixture is crumbly. Add water and mix all ingredients thoroughly. Pour into oiled fry-bake pan and stove-top bake until done, about 30 to 40 minutes.

GRAPE-NUT BREAD

1½ cups flour

1¼ cups Grape-Nuts

¼ cup brown sugar

2 Tbs. egg powder

1½ tsps. baking powder

¼ tsp. salt

½ tsp. cinnamon

3 Tbs. margarine

¼ cup dry milk

About 1¼ cups water

HELPFUL HINTS: Sauté the Grape-Nuts in margarine for about 5 minutes. Remove from heat and add sugar. Beat together the egg powder, dry milk, and water. Add the Grape-Nuts. Mix all the remaining dry ingredients and combine with the wet. Stove-top bake in oiled fry-bake pan until done, about 20 to 30 minutes.

Yeast Breads

Yeast . . . something that sometimes makes breads rise, a source of fear and loathing, certainly not to be considered when packing for the wilderness. Wait a minute . . . why not? Yeast wants to be your friend.

Yeast is a colony of minute fungi, living organisms, sleeping as dried flakes, powder, or cake. Warm water is needed to wake it up, and sugar is required to feed it while it grows. Yeast causes dough to rise by forming tiny pockets of carbon dioxide secondary to the fermentation of the sugar. Water should be very warm but not hot (you should be able to hold your finger in it, but just barely), and the sugar can be white, brown, molasses, honey, whatever you choose.

ESSENTIAL YEAST BREAD

1 pkg. yeast (1 Tbs.)

2 Tbs. sugar

1 tsp. salt (optional)

1¼ cups warm water

2 Tbs. oil or melted margarine (optional)
3 cups flour

HELPFUL HINTS: Combine the warm water, yeast, and sugar. (Some people like to add 1 teaspoon of salt and 1 or two tablespoons of oil. Some people don't.) We let the yeast begin its life in a prewarmed plastic, insulated mug to hold the heat. In about 5 to 10 minutes, the mass in the mug starts to bubble out the top; the yeast is fully awake and ready to use. Yeast is fragile during the first few minutes of awakening, and it will die if it gets too cold . . . or too hot. But once it's mixed with flour, it grows strong and hard to kill.

Put about 2 cups of flour in a pot, and add the activated yeast mixture. We like to mix wheat and white flour 50-50. Beat the mixture together with a spoon for 3 to 4 minutes, until it becomes a stringy mess. Add more flour slowly, kneading it into the mixture. Kneading can be done in the pot, in a frying pan, on a plastic bag, or on a foam-lite sleeping pad—wherever it's con-

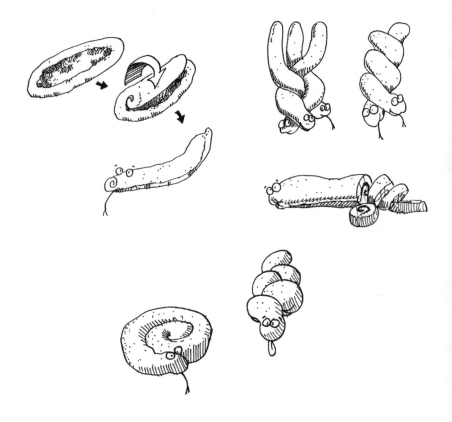

venient. Keep adding flour and kneading until a nonsticky ball of dough that holds its shape is formed. Total flour used will probably be about 3 cups.

Don't worry too much about your kneading style. We use the palms of our hands, folding the dough toward us and then turning the ends on top when it starts to get too narrow to comfortably work. Basically, dough likes a firm massage, so come up with your own method.

Plop the kneaded dough in a well-oiled, covered pot and set it in the sun to rise. If it's cold, we oil the surface of the doughball, put it in 2 plastic bags, and wear it inside our clothing until it rises. For fresh rolls in the morning, whip up the doughball at night, double-bag it, and sleep with it.

If you're in a hurry, dough doesn't have to rise to be used. The heat of baking will cause some rising. But the more it rises, the lighter and less dense the final product will be.

Before baking, knead the dough again for a few minutes, and place it in a well-oiled fry-bake pan. Stove-top bake, for a lighter yeast bread, or flip-bake, for a denser bread.

STYLE POINTS: Divide and roll your dough into snakes, then spiral, twist, or braid the snakes around your pan. Practice your knots with the snakes and bake them that way. For rolls, pinch off bits of the dough, roll them into balls, and pack them tightly into your fry-bake pan.

Popular Variations on the Theme

NUTRITION BOOST: Add 2–4 Tbs. egg powder and ½ cup dry milk to dry ingredients. Substitute ½ cup wheat germ or bran for ½ cup flour.

FRUIT AND NUT BREAD: Add handful of dried chopped fruit and nuts to dough before adding final cup of flour.

VEGETABLE BREAD: Add 1 Tbs. hydrated onion flakes, ½ tsp. garlic powder, ½ Tbs. parsley, and ½ cup hydrated smashed-up vegetables. Use a packet of bouillon instead of salt. Black pepper to taste. A handful of sunflower seeds is nice in this one, too.

MULTIGRAIN BREAD: Substitute ½ cup cooked grain for ½ cup flour. This is a great way to get rid of leftovers.

CHILI BREAD: Add 1 tsp. chili powder, 1 tsp. basil, and ¼ tsp. each garlic and cayenne. Top with cheese and/or beans.

RAISIN OATMEAL BREAD: Substitute ½ cup cooked oatmeal for ½ cup flour. Add ½ cup raisins and ½ tsp. cinnamon.

Truly Gourmet

SWEET CINNAMON BREAD

1 Essential Yeast Bread dough

2 tsps. cinnamon

½ cup brown sugar

Handful of raisins

Handful of nuts

HELPFUL HINTS: Proceed with Basic Yeast Bread recipe but, before you add the last cup of flour, add the extra ingredients.

Thanks to J. Scott McGee, Redmond, Oregon.

GARLIC HERB BREAD

1 Essential Yeast Bread dough

2 Tbs. herbs (oregano, basil, Italian, parsley, etc.)

2 fresh garlic cloves or 1 tsp. garlic powder

HELPFUL HINTS: Sauté garlic and herbs lightly in melted butter. Let cool and add before blending in last cup of flour. Proceed as in Essential Yeast Bread.

STYLE POINTS: Add ½ cup of Parmesan to dry ingredients. Just before you're ready to bake, press chunks of Swiss cheese into the dough about 1 inch apart. Stove-top bake.

Thanks to J. Scott McGee, Redmond, Oregon.

Desserts

No-Cooking-Required Desserts

PUDDING
(SERVES 2)

1 instant pudding mix
½ cup dry milk
2 cups cold water

HELPFUL HINTS: Don't add too much water. We like to shake the mix in a water bottle (45 seconds) or whisk it (1 to 2 minutes) and then secure it in a stream or snowbank to thicken. Makes a great rich shake or cake topping, too.

STYLE POINTS: Add leftover rice to pudding.

SNOW SHAKE

2 Tbs. egg powder
¼ cup dry milk
1 Tbs. sugar
1 tsp. vanilla
1 cup water

HELPFUL HINTS: Combine above ingredients thoroughly and add snow until mixture is thick and creamy.

STYLE POINTS: Leave out the sugar and add 2 to 3 tablespoons hot chocolate, pudding, or cheesecake mix.

SNOW CONES

#1: Mix fruit drink crystals or apple cider mix into a syrup. Pour over a mug of snow.

#2: Sprinkle fruit flavored gelatin over a mug of snow.

#3: Mix a mug full of snow with any of the syrups (see Breakfasts).

Limited-Cooking-Required Desserts

CHOCOLATE FONDUE

2 cups dry chocolate frosting mix

1 tsp. instant coffee or cinnamon and cloves to taste

4 Tbs. margarine

1 Tbs. dry milk

3 Tbs. water

HELPFUL HINTS: Melt margarine and combine all ingredients. Heat until hot but not boiling.

SERVING SUGGESTIONS: Dip with sweet bread, cake, graham crackers, vanilla wafers, marshmallows, fruit, or anything else you can find.

ALMOST PEANUT BUTTER CUPS
(MAKES 1 10-INCH ROUND)

³/₄ cup graham cracker or cookie crumbs

³/₄ cup peanut butter (crunchy is better)

¹/₂ lb. powdered sugar

¹/₄ cup margarine

1¹/₂ cups chocolate chips

HELPFUL HINTS: Melt margarine and mix in peanut butter, sugar, and crumbs. Press into bottom of fry-bake pan. Melt chips and pour them over crust. Chill for an hour or so, if you can wait that long.

STYLE POINTS *go to Tilda Musgrove, Live Oak, Florida.*

NO-BAKE PIE
(MAKES ONE 10-INCH PIE)

CRUST

1 cup graham cracker crumbs

3 Tbs. sugar

¹/₃ cup melted margarine

FILLING

1 instant pudding mix

¹/₂ cup dry milk

2 cups water

HELPFUL HINTS: You can buy Oreo, graham cracker, or ginger snap crumbs in the baking section of most supermarkets, or just carry them in your pack for a few days and let the job do itself. Melt margarine and combine it with the crumbs and sugar. If you're using cookie crumbs, leave out the sugar. Press mixture into the bottom of a frying pan. Make pudding in a bowl, or shake it in a water bottle. Pour over crust and set aside to chill.

FAVORITE COMBINATIONS

#1: Oreo crumbs and milk chocolate pudding.

#2: Ginger snap crumbs and tapioca.

#3: Graham cracker crumbs and banana or coconut pudding.

CHEESECAKE OR CHOCOLATE MOUSSE PIE
(MAKES ONE 8- TO 10-INCH PIE)

These mixes are commercially available packaged with directions and crust, but here are some general guidelines if you buy bulk or lose the directions.

CRUST: Mix crumbs with 3 Tbs. melted margarine. Press crumbs firmly into bottom of the pan. We like to sprinkle them on the top of filling for a quick, nonfrustrating option.

FILLING: Mix filling (about 1 cup) with ½ cup dry milk and about 1½ cups cold water. Beat with whisk or spoon until thick. Place on crust, cover, and set aside to chill.

STYLE POINTS: Top cheesecake with berry syrup.

MAINE NO-BAKE COOKIES
(SERVES 4–6)

3 cups quick oats

½ cup margarine

½ cup peanut butter

2 Tbs. dry milk

½ cup water

2 cups sugar

3 Tbs. cocoa

1 cup chopped nuts (optional)

HELPFUL HINTS: Bring margarine, milk, water, sugar, and cocoa to a boil. Remove from heat and mix in remaining ingredients. Press into bottom of a pan and set aside to cool. Cut and serve.

STYLE POINTS: While still warm, form the mixture into the shape of moose scat and, later, convince your companions that's what you are really eating. Be careful if you are traveling with children or you may find them sampling all kinds of wilderness excrement.

CREAMY RICE PUDDING
(SERVES 3–4)

1 cup instant rice

1½ cups water

2 Tbs. egg powder

⅓ cup dry milk

¼ cup brown sugar

¼ cup raisins

½ tsp. cinnamon or nutmeg

½ tsp. vanilla (optional)

HELPFUL HINTS: Combine all ingredients in a pan. Bring to a boil and simmer until rice and fruit are tender. Stir frequently, as this one likes to scorch. Add more water (preferably hot) if needed.

STYLE POINTS: Serve for breakfast. Or add ¼ cup or more hot chocolate for a chocolate dessert.

Baking-Required Desserts

GRAHAM CRACKER SURPRISE
(SERVES 4–6)

½ cup margarine

½ cup brown sugar

½ cup walnuts or pecans

8 graham crackers or their crumbs

HELPFUL HINTS: Mix margarine and sugar in a pan, and bring to a boil, stirring constantly. Place the graham crackers in the bottom of your fry-bake pan. Add the nuts to the boiling ooze and pour the mixture over graham crackers. Stove-top bake for about 10 minutes. Let the mixture cool and serve.

COFFEE BARS
(SERVES 4–6)

½ cup brown sugar

1½ cups Essential Batter Mix (see Backcountry Baking)

¼ cup oil

2 Tbs. egg powder

¾–1 cup strong warm coffee

1 tsp. vanilla (optional)

1 cup chocolate and nut bits

HELPFUL HINTS: Mix all ingredients and pour into an oiled fry-bake pan. Stove-top bake for about 30 minutes.

QUICK AND EASY CAKES

Carry a commercial cake and frosting mix. Most 10-inch fry-bake pans will accommodate only half a normal-sized cake mix (1½ to 2 cups). Remember to adjust for the altitude by adding flour and water (see Backcountry Baking).

ESSENTIAL CAKE MIX
(MAKES ONE 10-INCH-ROUND CAKE)

2 cups flour

¾ cup sugar

2½ tsps. baking powder

¼ cup egg powder (optional)

¼ cup milk powder

⅓ cup margarine

¼ tsp. salt (optional)

1 tsp. vanilla (optional)

1¼–1½ cups water

HELPFUL HINTS: Mix all dry ingredients and stir in the wet until batter is smooth. Pour into a well-oiled and floured fry-bake pan. Stove-top bake about 20 to 30 minutes.

Popular Variations on the Theme

CHOCOLATE CAKE: Add ¼ cup cocoa, an instant chocolate pudding, or ½ cup hot chocolate mix. Add more chocolate for a richer, darker cake.

CHOCOLATE BUTTERMILK CAKE: Make a chocolate cake (see above) and substitute dry buttermilk for dry milk.

SPICE CAKE: Add 1 tsp. cinnamon and ½ tsp. each nutmeg, cloves, and allspice. Include ¼ cup hydrated raisins and ¼ cup walnuts or pecans.

APPLESAUCE CAKE: Add 1 pkg. instant applesauce (Backpacker's Pantry), 1 tsp. cinnamon, ½ tsp. each cloves and allspice, ½ cup raisins, and ½ cup chopped nuts.

COCONUT PUDDING CAKE: Add an instant coconut pudding mix and cover with Coconut Hailstorm.

Truly Gourmet Cakes

PMS CAKE
(SERVES 4–6)

½ devil's food cake mix

½ pkg. instant chocolate pudding mix

½ cup dry milk

¼ cup egg powder

1¼ cups water

1 cup chocolate chips (or as many as you can pick out of the trail mix)

HELPFUL HINTS: Mix all ingredients until smooth. Pour into an oiled and floured fry-bake pan. Stove-top bake for 30 to 40 minutes.

FRUITY UPSIDE-DOWN CAKE
(MAKES ONE 10-INCH ROUND)

1–2 cups dried mixed fruit

1 cup chopped nuts

4–6 Tbs. sugar

3 Tbs. margarine

1 Essential Cake Mix batter with 1¼ cups water

HELPFUL HINTS: Hydrate fruit with some hot water (1 to 2 cups), margarine, and sugar in the bottom of your fry-bake pan. Add nuts. Follow recipe for

Essential Cake Batter. Pour mixture over the top of the fruit. Stove-top bake until done, 20 to 30 minutes.

STYLE POINTS: Use apricots and pecans with a chocolate cake. Top with caramel icing.

CRAZY MIXED-UP BOSTON CREAM PIE
(MAKES ONE 10-INCH ROUND)

1 Basic Cake Mix batter with 1 1/4 cups water

1 instant vanilla pudding mix

1/2 cup dry milk and 2 cups cold water

1 cup chocolate chips

HELPFUL HINTS: Stove-top bake 1 Essential Cake Mix batter. Prepare 1 instant vanilla pudding mix and set aside to chill. When cake is done, sprinkle with chocolate chips, cover, and set aside for chips to melt. Cover with pudding and serve.

Frostings, Icings, and a Few Hailstorms

QUICK TOPPINGS

#1: Carry frosting mix. They come in just-add-water varieties.

#2: Chocolate, carob, or butterscotch chips: After cake is done, scatter chips on the top, cover, and set aside until chips melt. Peppermint patties work great too, but you'll need to spread them after they soften.

#3: Instant pudding topping: Make pudding first. Set it aside to chill while you bake the cake. Spread on top of cooled cake.

#4: Cover cake with one of the syrups or butters (see Breakfasts).

#5: Sprinkle cake with powdered sugar or cinnamon sugar.

COCONUT HAILSTORM

1 1/2 cups coconut flakes

1/3 cup brown sugar

1/3 cup soft margarine

2 Tbs. dry milk or buttermilk

1/2 tsp. vanilla

1/4 cup water

HELPFUL HINTS: Combine all ingredients, spread over top of warm cake, and cover until melted.

STYLE POINTS: Build a small twiggy fire on top of the oven to brown coconut.

ESSENTIAL FROSTING I

1 Tbs. dry milk
2 Tbs. flour
1/4 cup margarine
1/4 cup sugar
1/4 cup water
1/2 tsp. vanilla

HELPFUL HINTS: Heat flour, dry milk, and water until very thick. Set aside to cool. Add sugar, margarine, and vanilla. Whip with wire whisk or spoon until thick. A whisk is really useful with this one.

ESSENTIAL FROSTING II

1 1/2 cups powdered sugar
1/4 cup soft margarine
1/2 tsp. vanilla
1 Tbs. dry milk
2 Tbs. water

HELPFUL HINTS: Combine dry and then add wet ingredients slowly. It really doesn't take much water, so be careful.

Popular Variations on the Frosting Theme

CHOCOLATE SAUCE: Add 2 Tbs. cocoa or 1/4 cup hot chocolate mix.

MOCHA SAUCE: Add 2 Tbs. cocoa and substitute coffee for water.

SPICE FROSTING: Add 1/2 tsp. cinnamon and a sprinkle of nutmeg and cloves.

Truly Gourmet Frostings

INTERNATIONAL FROSTING: Add 1/4 cup of any of the instant International Coffees to Basic Frosting I or II. Café Français is a particular hit.

Thanks go to Jennifer Gray Rouillard, Cincinnati, Ohio, who had to take three planes to figure this one out.

CARAMEL ICING

1 cup sugar

5 Tbs. soft margarine

2 Tbs. dry milk

1/3 cup water

1 tsp. vanilla (optional)

HELPFUL HINTS: Combine sugar, milk, and water in a pan. Bring to a boil, stirring constantly. Cook until a soft ball starts to form. Remove from heat. Add margarine and vanilla. Beat until creamy. If it's too thick, thin by adding water 1 teaspoon at a time. If it's too thin, add flour.

STYLE POINTS: Thin out the frosting by adding water. Poke holes in the cake and pour the icing over the top.

RICH FUDGE FROSTING

1 1/2 cups sugar

1/3 cup cocoa or 3/4 cup hot chocolate mix

3–4 Tbs. dry milk

2 Tbs. margarine

1/2 tsp. vanilla (optional)

3/4 cup water

HELPFUL HINTS: Combine sugar, milk, water, and cocoa in a pan. Cook over medium heat, stirring constantly, until mixture comes to a boil. Boil, stirring very occasionally (only to prevent sticking), until mixture thickens and will become syrup when dropped in cold water. (Try a little drop occasionally in your mug.) At this point, remove from heat, add margarine and vanilla, and cool until lukewarm. Beat with spoon until fudge thickens and quickly spread it on cake.

STYLE POINTS: Double the recipe. Spread in a pan and serve as fudge after it cools.

PEANUT BUTTER FROSTING

2 Tbs. peanut butter

1 1/2 cups powdered sugar

1 Tbs. dry milk

2–3 Tbs. water

HELPFUL HINTS: Cream all ingredients together and spread on cooled cake.

Crisps, Cobblers, and Pies

CRISPY FRUIT CRUNCH

(SERVES 4–6)

2 cups fruit (dried, or any type of edible berry is scrumptious)

1/2 cup raisins

1/2 cup nut bits

1/2 cup quick oatmeal

1/4 cup flour

1/4 cup brown sugar

1–2 cups reconstituted orange drink (use water and sugar as an option)

1/4 cup margarine

1/2 tsp. cinnamon

HELPFUL HINTS: Combine fruit or wild berries (use less fluid if using fresh versus dried fruit or berries) and orange drink in bottom of fry-bake pan. Bring to a boil and set aside, covered. Combine remaining ingredients and spread evenly over fruit. Stove-top bake until crisp, about 20 minutes.

WILD CURRANT COTTLESTONE PIE

(SERVES 4–6)

2 cups currants (or any other edible berry)

1 cup flour

1/2 cup sugar

1 1/2 tsps. baking powder

3 Tbs. milk powder

3/4 cup water

2 Tbs. margarine

HELPFUL HINTS: Combine flour, sugar, baking powder, and milk in a pan. Add water and mix until the batter is smooth. Melt margarine in bottom of fry-bake pan. Pour in batter. Pile berries on top. Stove-top bake until done.

Thanks go to Tim Lindholm, Boulder, Colorado.

APPLE COBBLER

(SERVES 4–6)

2 cups dried apples

2 Tbs. margarine

1/4 cup brown sugar

1/2 tsp. cinnamon

1 1/2 cups water

1 cup Essential Batter Mix (see Backcountry Baking)

1/2 cup oatmeal or flour (we prefer oatmeal)

HELPFUL HINTS: Combine apples, sugar, margarine, cinnamon, and water in a fry-bake pan. Bring to a boil and simmer until fruit is tender. Meanwhile, mix oatmeal and Essential Batter Mix into a stiff batter. Spoon mixture onto tender fruit and stove-top bake until dough is brown.

ESSENTIAL PIECRUST

(MAKES ONE 9- TO 10-INCH CRUST)

1 1/3 cups flour

1/3 cup margarine

3–4 Tbs. cold water

1 Tbs. dry milk

HELPFUL HINTS: Combine all ingredients and work into a ball. Press dough into the bottom and sides of a fry-bake pan.

STYLE POINTS: Double recipe for double-crust pie.

RAISIN PIE

(MAKES ONE 10-INCH PIE)

1 Essential Piecrust

1 1/2 cups raisins

1 1/2 cups water

1/3 cup sugar

2 Tbs. flour

1 cup chopped nuts

1 tsp. cinnamon

1/2 tsp. cloves (optional)

HELPFUL HINTS: Simmer raisins in water until tender. Add sugar and flour and boil for 1 minute. Add nuts and spices. Spoon onto pie shell. Stove-top bake until shell is done, about 20 minutes.

APPLE PIE

(MAKES ONE 10-INCH PIE)

1 Essential Piecrust

FILLING

1 1/2 cups chopped dried apples

1/2 cup raisins

2 Tbs. flour

1/2 cup sugar

2 cups water

TOPPING

1/2 cup brown sugar

1 tsp. cinnamon

2 Tbs. butter

1/2 cup chopped nuts

2 Tbs. oatmeal

HELPFUL HINTS: Simmer apples, raisins, and water until tender. Add sugar and flour and boil 1 minute. Pour into pie shell. Mix all topping ingredients together and crumble onto top of apple mixture. Stove-top bake until crust is done, about 20 minutes.

Coffee and
Other Addictions

ot drinks should be a part of your backcountry diet: They warm you. Most of them energize you. They are a pleasant way to stall while meals cook. They make you more socially acceptable—or at least there's a chance they will. They hydrate you (if the caffeine content isn't too high).

Caffeine opens your eyes, sharpens your mind, lifts your mood, increases endurance, hides tiredness, and hones your senses to a hair-splitting edge. It also makes your hands shake, increases your heart rate, keeps you awake, ups your stomach acid and your need to urinate, and stains your teeth. So what. We can't imagine a backcountry morning (or any morning) without coffee. Coffee, if you're worried, has no connection with heart disease, benign or malignant cancers, or any other illness. If you drink too much caffeine for too long, you'll have withdrawal symptoms when you can't find any: headache, lethargy, anxiety, irritability. But two or three cups a day are a boon, a blessing, a gift from the gods.

YIPPEE-KI-YAY COWBOY COFFEE

Mini espresso machines and backcountry percolators are nice and unnecessary . . . even though we sometimes use them. All you really need is an old pot and lots of ground coffee beans. For every cup of water in the pot, approximately, put in 1 heaping Tbs. of coffee, approximately. Always throw in a little extra coffee . . . for the pot. Put the pot on the stove and watch it impatiently. A watched pot never boils, which is why you watch it. Boiling coffee makes it bitter. Just as the black water starts to move around under its own power, take it off the stove, cover the pot, and wait a few minutes for the grounds to settle. Pour off a steaming cup while unsuccessfully trying to keep all the grounds in the pot. Later you spit out the grounds that work their way into your mouth. This is a necessary and treasured aspect of cowboy coffee. If you choke a little on the first and last swallow, it's probably just right.

CHEATER'S COFFEE

Manufacturers such as Brother's put very good ground coffee in a single-serving, tea-style bag. Put the bag in your insulated travel mug and fill the mug with boiling water. Snap on the mug's lid and wait about 5 minutes while the coffee steeps. It ain't cowboy coffee, but it ain't bad. If you tear the bag open—accidentally or on purpose—you still get to spit grounds. Many stores carry Singlebrew coffee bags or similar products.

HOT CHOCOLATE

Some people, surprisingly, prefer the taste of chocolate to the taste of coffee. Save yourself a lot of bother and buy the kind of instant hot chocolate that requires no added milk. A strong cup of hot chocolate provides about as much caffeine as a weak cup of instant coffee. Hot chocolate has plenty of sugar for energy.

Then there are those people who like to mix hot chocolate and coffee. These people are usually indecisive, but the resulting brew is not bad. For the truly lazy, General Foods offers International Coffees, instant flavored mixes with a very acceptable taste, sort of like premixed hot-chocolate-and-coffee for cheaters.

TEA

As all good residents of the British Isles know, afternoon and evening is the time for tea. Tea is a fine settling-down drink. We prefer noncaffeine herbal teas, which settle you down more than teas with caffeine.

OPTIONS

Flavorful, hydrating energy boosts can be provided by drinking hot several beverages that come in powders and are not usually thought of as a hot drink: Jell-O, Tang Instant Breakfast Drink, apple cider, lemonade. When it comes to hot drink options, you're limited by only your imagination and your ability to heat water.

Appendix

Cups per Pound of Commonly Packed Foods

FOOD (1 POUND)	MEASURE
Almonds, shelled	3½ cups
Apples, dried	4–5 cups
Apricots, dried	3½ cups
Barley, pearled	2 cups
Beans, black, instant	4¾ cups
Biscuit mix	3⅔ cups, lightly packed
Butter	2 cups
Bulgur	2⅔ cups
Cashews	3¼ cups
Cheese, Parmesan, grated	5⅓ cups
Chocolate chips	2½ cups
Cocoa powder	4 cups
Coconut, dried	4 cups
Cornmeal	3 cups
Couscous	2⅔ cups
Cream of wheat	3 cups
Eggs, dried	4 cups
Falafel, instant	3¼ cups
Farina	3 cups
Fruit drinks	3 cups
Flour	4 cups
Gelatin, flavored	2⅓ cups
Grits, dry	3 cups
Honey	1½ cups
Hot chocolate, instant	4 cups
Hummus, instant powder	4 cups
Lentils	2¼ cups

FOOD (1 POUND)	MEASURE
Macaroni	3½–4 cups
Nonfat dry milk	4 cups
Noodles, egg	8–9 cups
Oatmeal	5 cups
Peaches, dried	3 cups
Peanut butter	1⅔ cups
Peas, dried split	2⅓ cups
Peaches, dried	3 cups
Peanuts, shelled	3 cups
Pecans, shelled	3 cups
Potato flakes	6 cups
Pudding mix	3 cups
Raisins	3 cups, packed
Refries, instant powdered	3½ cups
Rice	3 cups
Rice, instant	9 cups
Rice, wild	2 cups
Sesame seeds	4 cups
Sugar	2¼ cups
Sugar, brown	3 cups, firmly packed
Sugar, powdered	4 cups
Sunflower seeds	3½–4 cups
Tomatoes, dry flakes	2¾ cups
Vegetables, dried	5–6 cups
Walnuts	4 cups
Wheat germ	4 cups
Wheat bran	4 cups

Substitutions

1 tsp.	baking powder	equals	¼ tsp. baking soda + ½ tsp. cream of tartar
1 Tbs.	bouillon	equals	1 bouillon cube
1 cup	margarine	equals	⅞ cup vegetable oil
1 tsp.	mustard powder	equals	1 tsp. mustard, Dijon
1 tsp.	onion powder	equals	¼ cup onion, fresh minced
1 tsp.	onion, minced dried	equals	¼ onion, fresh minced
⅓ cup	pepper, sweet flakes	equals	1 fresh pepper
1 Tbs.	cornstarch	equals	2 Tbs. flour
2 Tbs.	egg, powdered	equals	1 egg + 2 Tbs. water
½ cup	fruit, dried	equals	1 fresh medium-sized fruit
1 clove	garlic	equals	⅛ tsp. garlic powder
1 Tbs.	herbs, fresh	equals	½ tsp. herbs, dried
⅔ cup	honey	equals	1 cup sugar
1 cup	milk	equals	¼ cup dried whole milk + 1 cup water

Measurements

IS EQUIVALENT TO:

Dash . . . . less than ⅛ tsp.

3 tsp . . . . 1 Tbs.

4 Tbs. . . . . ¼ cup or 2 fl. oz.

8 Tbs. . . . . ½ cup or 4 fl. oz.

16 Tbs . . . . 1 cup or 8 fl. oz.

2 cups . . . . 1 pt. or 16 fl. oz. or 1 lb.

4 cups . . . . 1 qt. or 32 fl. oz.

2 pts . . . . 1 qt.

4 qts . . . . 1 gal.

16 oz. . . . . 1 lb.

1 liter . . . . 1,000 ml.

1 liter (.946) . . . . 1 qt.

½ liter (.47) . . . . 1 pt.

1 gallon of water . . . . 8 lbs.

1 12-oz. travel mug . . . . 1½ cups if filled to lip

Calories per Pound of Commonly Used Foods

BREAKFAST	Calories/lb.
Cream of wheat	1,658
Granola	2,211
Grape-Nuts	1,760
Hash browns—dry	1,600
Oatmeal	1,672
Wheatena	1,618

DINNERS	
Bulgur	1,621
Couscous	1,600
Egg noodles	1,760
Falafel	2,200
Lentils	1,860
Macaroni	1,674
Potatoes—sliced	1,624
Potato flakes	1,650
Refried beans	2,200
Rice	1,647
Spaghetti	1,674
Tortillas	1,200

FLOUR	
Bisquick	1,920
Cornmeal	1,610
Muffin mix	2,280
Sweet bread mix	2,000
White	1,650
Wheat	1,651

HIGH-CALORIE (HIGH-FAT) ITEMS	
Cheddar	1,840
Cream cheese	1,600
Mozzarella whole milk	1,280
Parmesan	2,080
Swiss	1,680
Sour cream	1,600
Margarine	3,200
Oil	4,000
Bacon pieces	2,836
Ham	1,800
Peanut butter	2,682
Pepperoni	2,255
Salami	2,041
Smoked salmon	800
Tuna, "water packed"	720
Tuna, "oil packed"	880
TVP	1,500

TRAIL FOOD	
Apples	1,102
Apricots	1,080
Bagels	1,800
Candy—hard	1,751
Cashews	2,604
Chocolate bars	1,650
Crackers	1,828
Coconut	2,468
Dates	1,243
Fruit bars	3,000
Mixed nuts	2,694
M&Ms	2,100
Pita bread	1,000
Peanuts	2,558
Popcorn	1,642
Power Bars	1,600
Raisins	1,360
Sunflower seeds	2,550
Trail mix	2,000
Walnuts	2,950

DRINKS AND SUGAR	
Brown sugar	1,700
Fruit crystals	1,950
Gatorade	1,600
Honey	1,379
Hot chocolate	2,000
Jell-O	1,683
White sugar	1,700

DESSERT	
Brownie mix	1,828
Cake mix	2,200
Cheesecake mix	3,500
Gingerbread mix	1,928
Pudding	1,637

MISCELLANEOUS	
Chicken base	1,117
Beef base	1,082
Corn—dried	1,600
Instant soups: 1 cup	100
Eggs, powdered	2,697
Milk—dried, nonfat	1,625
Peas and carrots—dried	1,200
Peas and onions—dried	1,200
Peppers—dried	1,000
Ramen soup	1,067
Soup mix—veggie	1,600
Tomato base	1,350

Note: Most of these products can be ordered, or at least researched, from the comfort of the chair in front of your computer.

Sources of Food and Gear

Just Add Water: Freeze-Dried and Dehydrated Foods

Adventure Foods, 481 Banjo Lane, Whittier, NC 28789. 1–828–497–4113. (www.adventurefoods.com)

AlpineAire Foods, P.O. Box 926, Nevada City, CA 95959. 1–800–322–6325. (www.alpineairefoods.com)

Backpacker's Pantry, 6350 Gunpark Drive, Boulder, CO 80301-3337. 1–800–641–0500. (www.backpackerspantry.com)

Chamy Snacks, 117 West Denny Way #216, Seattle, WA 98119. 1–800–322–7010.

Harvest Foodworks, Ltd., 445 Highway 29, Tuledo, Ontario K0E 1Y0. 1–800–268–4268. (www.harvest.on.ca)

Mountain Safety Research, P.O. Box 24547, Seattle, WA 98124. 1–800–877–9677. (www.msrcorp.com) (EcoCuisine)

Oregon Freeze Dry, Inc., P.O. Box 1048, Albany, OR 97321. 1–800–547–4060. (www.mountainhouse.com) (Mountain House)

Richmoor Corporation, P.O. Box 8092, Van Nuys, CA 91409. 1–800–423–3170. (www.richmoor.com) (Natural High)

Sorrenti Family Farms, 1725 Main Street, Escalon, CA 95320. 1–209–838–1127.

Trail Gourmet, Inc., P.O. Box 167, Amherst, OH 44001. 1–440–365–3740. (www.TrailGourmet.com)

High-Energy Drinks and Bars

AlpineAire Foods, P.O. Box 926, Nevada City, CA 95959. 1–800–322–6325. (www.alpineairefoods.com) (E-mergen-C)

Balance Bar Company, 1015 Mark Avenue, Carpinteria, CA 93013. 1–800–678–4246. (www.balance.com)

Clif Bar, Inc., 1610 5th Street, Berkeley, CA 94710. 1–800–884–5254. (www.clifbar.com)

Champion Nutrition, 2615 Stanwell Drive, Concord, CA 94520. 1–800–225–4831. (www.champion-nutrition.com) (Revenge Energy Drink)

Gatorade Company, P.O. Box 049003, Chicago, IL 60604-9003.
(www.gatorade.com)

Optim Nutrition, 2401 South Foothill Drive, Salt Lake City, UT 84109.
1-800-865-3134. (www.mountainlift.com) (Mountain Lift Bar)

PowerFood, Inc., 1442A Walnut Street, Berkeley, CA 94709.
1-800-587-6937. (www.powerbar.com)

SportPharma, 1915 Mark Court, Suite 150, Concord, CA 94520.
1-800-654-4246. (www.sportpharma.com) (Promax Bar)

Sqwincher Corp., P.O. Box 8250, Columbus, MS 39705. 1-800-654-1920.
(www.sqwincher.com)

Weider Food Companies, 2002 South 5070 West, Salt Lake City, UT 84104.
1-800-695-7888. (Tiger Sport Bar)

Stoves and Fuel

A&H Industries, Box 101, La Mirada, CA 90637-0101. 1-888-456-0748.
(www.packstoves.com) (Camping Gaz, Optimus, Primus: sales and
service)

Black Diamond Equipment, Ltd., 2084 East 3900 South, Salt Lake City,
UT 84124. 1-801-278-5533. (www.bibler.com) (Bibler Hanging Stove)

Coleman Company, P.O. Box 2931, Wichita, KS 67201. 1-800-835-3278.
(www.coleman.com) (Stoves and fuel; call or write for the nearest
dealer)

Mountain Safety Research (MSR), P.O. Box 24547, Seattle, WA 98124.
1-800-877-9677. (www.msrcorp.com) (XGK, WhisperLite, DragonFly,
SuperFly, RapidFire)

Suunto, 2151 Las Palmas Drive, Suite G, Carlsbad, CA 92009.
1-800-543-9124. (www.suuntousa.com) (Primus)

Gear for the Outdoor Kitchen

Atwater Carey, Ltd., 339 East Rainbow Boulevard, Salida, CO 81201.
1-800-359-1646. (www.destinationoutdoors.com) (Campside Kitchen
and Campside Jr.)

Backpacker's Pantry, 6350 Gunpark Drive, Boulder, CO 80301-3337.
1-800-641-0500. (www.backpackerspantry.com) (Cookware, Outback
Oven)

Banks Fry-Bake Company, P.O. Box 183, Claverack, NY 12513.
1-888-FRY-BAKE. (www.frybake.com)

Mountain Safety Research (MSR), P.O. Box 24547, Seattle, WA 98124. 1-800-877-9677. (www.msrcorp.com) (Cookware)

Outdoor Research, 2203 First Avenue South, Seattle, WA 98134-1424. 1-888-4-ORGEAR. (www.orgear.com) (Kitchen Kits: Solo, Hiker, Back-packer, Camper)

Stansport, 2801 East 12th Street, Los Angeles, CA 90023. 1-800-421-6131. (www.stansport.com) (Cookware)

Strike 2 Industries, Inc., East 508 Augusta Avenue, Spokane, WA 99207. 1-509-484-3701. (BakePacker)

Water Filters

Cascade Designs, Inc., 4000 1st Avenue South, Seattle, WA 98134. 1-800-531-9531. (www.cascadedesigns.com) (SweetWater, Guardian+Plus)

General Ecology, 151 Sheree Boulevard, Exton, PA 19341. 1-800-441-8166. (www.generalecology.com) (First Need Deluxe)

Mountain Safety Research (MSR), Box 24547, Seattle, WA 98124. 1-800-877-9677. (www.msrcorp.com) (WaterWorks II and MiniWorks)

Recovery Engineering, 2229 Edgewood Avenue South, Minneapolis, MN 55426. 1-800-845-7873. (www.purwater.com) (PUR Explorer, Scout, and Voyageur)

Suunto, 2151 Las Palmas Drive, Suite G, Carlsbad, CA 92009. 1-800-543-9124. (www.suuntousa.com) (Katadyn Pocket and Mini)

One-Stop Shopping: Everything You Could Possibly Need and More

Campmor, 810 Route 17 North, Paramus, NJ 07653-0999. 1-800-CAMP-MOR. (www.campmor.com)

Colorado Adventure & Medical Products, P.O. Box 16651, Denver, CO 80216. 1-800-916-CAMP. (www.campstuff.com)

Eastern Mountain Sports (EMS), 1 Vose Farm Road, Peterborough, NH 03458. 1-888-INFO-EMS. (www.easternmountainsports.com)

L. L. Bean, 5381 Main Street, Freeport, ME 04033. 1-800-543-9089. (www.llbean.com)

Recreational Equipment, Inc. (REI), P.O. Box 88125, Seattle, WA 98138. 1-800-426-4840. (www.rei.com)

Index

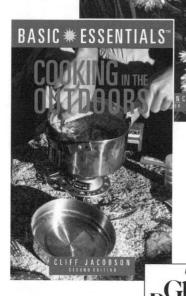